One More Sunset

One More Sunset

A True Story of Survival through Commitment, Trust and Love

Penny,

May you Enjoy All your Sunset —

Best Wishes

Jimmy —

2-25-10

Jim Connelly

edited by Kate Connelly and Paula Sarcona

Never give up...

printed by Ave Maria Press

International Standard Book Number: 0-9708387-0-0

Edited by Kate Connelly and Paula Sarcona

Cover and text design by Katherine Robinson Coleman

Printed by Ave Maria Press, Inc., P.O. Box 428, Notre Dame, IN 46556

First Edition

DEDICATION

This book is dedicated to Kate Kelly Connelly for her love, understanding and support. For those who are lucky enough to know her, the reasons are obvious. For those who don't, let me explain.

Kate came into my life when there appeared to be very little left of it. I was in the middle of a minefield, immobilized and carrying a heavy load down a long, dark road.

Her understanding of long-term care, her compassion for the injured person I had taken into my life and her own history as a caregiver brought great comfort to me in a time of need. It was her patience, knowledge, experience and—most of all—her love that enabled me to continue my commitment.

In short, Kate made the difference.

I also dedicate this book to my son and partner Jeff Connelly from whom I have learned grace and balance, and for his support of me and my continued commitment to Donna.

And for my daughter Katy Clare, I dedicate this book in hopes that I have set the example to never give up. May she always see the glass half full and that it is not what happens to you in life but what you do about it that matters.

JIM CONNELLY

CONTENTS

ACKNOWLEDGMENTS

Praise for the People
Who Helped

When thinking of the many people who are responsible for aiding in Donna's recovery, *thank you* seems so inadequate. But with a very grateful heart, I say thanks first of all to Donna for committing totally to her own recovery, for trusting me and loving life enough to fight the fight of her life. I have learned so much from her courage; to Jean Jones, Donna's mother, for entrusting the Connelly family with her daughter; to the rescue team from Sealey Lake, Montana, Rick Hawthorne and Roger Watson who kept her alive; to Geri Watson for her help in getting me out to the accident; to the helicopter pilot who took enormous risk to pick Donna up off the ice in the dark of the night; to Dr. Roth and his staff at St. Patrick's Hospital in Missoula, Montana; to Dr. Barry Ludwig, a noted neurologist and the most positive doctor I know, who encouraged us to "keep doing what you are doing"; to the staff at Daniel Freeman Hospital, Inglewood, California; to the Pastoral Care Division of Daniel Freeman Hospital, especially the nuns who "adopted" Donna and always made time for her; to Rob Gianelli, my friend and attorney who was unselfish and kind enough to bring in an extraordinary attorney, Tim Wheeler, to represent Donna when we had to take legal

9

action against the snowmobile manufacturer; to Tim Wheeler who fought the tough five-year fight against the most powerful and prevailed on Donna's behalf. Because of his knowledge, integrity and drive, Donna receives lifetime compensation on a monthly basis. Tim, as a courtesy to our friendship and out of concern for Donna's future, refused to take the normal attorney's fee. Tim was with Donna and me every step of the way; to attorney Sally Friedman for her friendship and stewardship through the courts and the conservatorship; to attorney Bob Masenga who assisted with a number of mandatory court appearances, always with a smile; to Margo Bach and her staff who provided Donna with invaluable one-on-one life skills therapy; to Harry Murphy and Steve Love of Cal State Northridge, leaders in the field of education of challenged individuals, who encouraged me and Donna to not give up and find a way for Donna to go back to school; to Dr. Bates, Dr. Starr, Dr. Clark and Dr. Gerson for their sensitivity to Donna's challenges in the early years of her recovery; to Christy and Ron Cluff for their continual encouragement; to Sue Erickson, Donna's Kodak co-worker and long-time friend; to Nancy Clement, Donna's best friend and cheerleading partner in high school; to Liva Yates, Irene Kolman, Ron Keibort, Wayne Reeder, Jaimie Simon, Richard Fleming and Jill Clemence for quality time spent with Donna; to Alice Dandridge, Vinetta Tolbert, Joe Wolf, Rick, Mike, Josh and Tony for taking special care of Donna while driving her from place to place; to Joan MacClellan, Donna's landlord, who has seen to it that Donna has been safe and warm in her home; to Paul Silva, writer for the *Beach Reporter* and to John Bogert, writer for the *Daily Breeze*, both who made the community aware of Donna's story and helped Donna integrate into the community because of their fine articles; to Marguerite Ris, a dear friend from Switzerland, who brought joy and encouragement to Donna, and to Tracy and Karen from Orange County, who visited Donna regularly; to Flo and the Seniors who cared for Donna, especially on the Senior trips; to Keyo and Vince at Manhattan Photo, who share Donna's adventure through pictures; to Steve Murillo, a Manhattan Beach entrepreneur who opened his office and heart to Donna for a magnificent birthday party; to Lee and Lisa, owners of Growing Wild, and their assistant, Scotty, who are always kind and encouraging and who share their beautiful flowers with Donna; to George at Whale of a Wash for his friendship with Donna and keeping her in clean clothes; to T.J. Kelly, my wife's brother, for taking such good care of Donna by providing her with Reebok shoes and clothes; to all the wonderful people in Manhattan Beach who have been so kind and understanding throughout the years; to Jack Sarcona, Ann Banks, Catherine Lurie, Michelle Mervosh, Jeff at the Kettle, Harriett Chase, to our long-time friend, Rudy Reutigger, for his encouragement and support during Donna's recovery; to my childhood friends, Rich Bartulski and Jack Rainaldi, for always going that extra mile for Donna; to my dear friends Roy and Betty Noble for their continuing and uninterrupted support and care of Donna; to Kathy McGowan for her encouragement, support, knowledge and endless amounts of time that she gave to me to complete this book; to Paula Sarcona, who in 1994 God sent when the light at the end of the tunnel was dimming, who continues to have a major impact on Donna and all of our lives in a very positive way; to my mother, Clare, my sister Kathe, my sister Angela and her husband Hugh for their generous gifts of time and love; for unselfishly rearranging their lives, for being there at the beginning and the end, always there to support and step in when needed; to my wife, Kate, and daughter, Katy Clare, who have loved us both and made Donna a part of our family.

When I was asked to write the foreword for the book *One More Sunset*, I thought what could I possibly add to this manuscript. However, because Jim Connelly is a friend and I have met Donna and am aware of her difficult experience, I consented to consider it. Even then, I thought I couldn't do this because of the time constraints placed on me by my busy schedule. However, after reading this book, I couldn't possibly say no. As a matter of fact, it is a privilege to write this foreword.

Less than three years ago, my wife, Beth, was diagnosed with throat cancer and she was given a 10% chance to live one year. The cancer was in stage IV when she underwent 12 hours of surgery and 83 radiation treatments. Her weight went down to 89 pounds. She and I had no idea what the next day would bring. We talked to Brett Butler and many others who had the same type of surgery. We read every book we could get hold of in an attempt to understand what thoughts and emotions the other person was experiencing.

My wife has made a miraculous recovery thanks to the numerous prayers offered on her behalf by so many people around the country in general and the Notre Dame family in particular. There isn't a month that goes by that we don't receive a phone call from a family who is presently undergoing the same experiences as we had. We always accommodate their requests willingly in the hope we can alleviate some of their concerns.

As in our own search for answers, I feel one of the valuable assets of this book is that it will give all of us a better understanding of the emotions and concerns an individual and their family experiences when they suffer a disability, injury or illness.

This book is a true story of a courageous young lady named Donna Jones who had a bright future with Kodak until she was seriously injured in a snowmobile accident. After being in a coma for 48 days, Donna fought a courageous battle, and I am sure you will be impressed with her determination to never give up.

As I read this book I also was appalled that people could be so cruel to somebody in a time of need. I know I will be far more tolerant and considerate in the future.

When we are faced with difficulty, I believe God sends a guardian angel to help us. Jim Connelly was this angel for Donna. I have known Jim since my days as the football coach at Notre Dame. Over the years he has been a great friend. I select my friends based on three questions. Can I trust them? Are they committed to excellence? Do they care about other people? Jim always scored high in all three categories.

Jim's, and his wife, Kate's, dedication to helping Donna recover is a marvelous example for all of us to follow. Jim not only financed the majority of Donna's expenses (which were substantial), he gave her his time and emotional support. I would hope I could be such a friend when God calls me to do so.

Obviously, there were many times when Jim and Donna's relationship became testy and argumentative. However, Donna's courage and Jim's genuine caring for people enabled them to overcome all obstacles. As you read this, I think you will be impressed with Jim's intolerance of anyone, including doctors, who may not have exhibited his commitment to excellence and shared his positive attitude.

This book is easy to read. It is moving, uplifting and causes you to reflect on how you would react if you were in Jim's or Donna's situation.

In closing, I hope after reading this book your reaction will be the same as mine. It was so moving I gave it to a friend who is recovering from a serious accident. They read it and thanked me.

LOU HOLTZ

CHAPTER 1

From Pots and Pans to the Big League

There are times in life that are unforgettable, moments that forever remain in our memories. For Donna Jones, a mid-winter afternoon in 1982 at the Orange County, California offices of Eastman Kodak was such a time. During a sales meeting that day, Donna was announced as the winner of a trip to Las Vegas for two, all expenses paid. She had won many small contests before at Kodak, but this one was the ultimate. In many ways, it marked the turning point in her young career.

Donna had worked for Kodak since the summer break between her junior and senior years at Boston College in Massachusetts. Kodak wasn't her first job, however. Her college summers were all spent earning money, partly because of her unceasing energy and drive but mainly out of necessity. In 1972, during her final year in high school, her father died.

Donna wanted desperately to attend college, but her mother now had the responsibility of four children to support. In addition to Donna, there were two sons, Jimmy and Tommy, and another daughter, Carolyn.

For a time it seemed college would be little more than a dream, but Donna was determined. An excellent student, a cheerleader, and active in school and community activities, she applied for dozens of scholarships and sent applications to several colleges and universities. She received offers from all of the schools and ultimately settled on her first choice.

Donna enrolled at Springfield College in Springfield, Mass., as a physical education major. She loved all sports, but swimming was her favorite. During the summer of 1974, she worked as a camp counselor, earning $250.00 over the three-month period. It was a great job, she thought, until she discovered she could make a lot more money selling EKCO cookware. The following summer she earned $250.00 a day going door-to-door with pots and pans. "Forget the gym stuff," she told friends. "I'm going into business!"

At the end of her sophomore year at Springfield, Donna transferred to Boston College on scholarship. As part of a marketing class, she was asked to address her fellow students. She eagerly accepted. For 20 minutes, Donna stood before her class and talked about her experiences selling cookware, the challenges of working with the public, and the joys in closing a sale. Her professor was so impressed he offered words of advice. "If you like selling," he told her, "apply to Kodak. They have a summer program."

An interviewer came to campus and Donna was hired on the spot. She was one of only 30 students from across the country hired by Kodak for the summer.

The job was tailor-made for Donna. Traveling to department stores and camera shops in New York, New Jersey and Connecticut, she demonstrated Kodak products to potential customers. She was a natural and she excelled at it. Wherever she went people were drawn to her outgoing personality and ready smile. In addition, she was chosen to call on the national parks in the western United States. She couldn't imagine a more perfect assignment because she loved to travel and thrived on new adventures.

Donna had counted on working full-time for Kodak upon her graduation from Boston College in

18

1977, but Kodak announced a freeze on hiring that year. Disappointed, she reluctantly took a job with a pharmaceutical firm headquartered in Houston and began training to sell medical supplies to doctors. In her heart, she knew it was only an interim job. Fortunately, she was assigned a territory in Boston, closer to home.

Upon her return east she wasted no time in contacting Kodak. She wanted not only to stay in touch with her friends there but to let them know how much she wanted to come back to Kodak. To her surprise, she was told, "Your timing is perfect." Kodak had an opening for a lead demonstrator to train in-store help on setting up displays and the use of Kodak's new Instant Camera. If she wanted the job she had only to go to Kodak's headquarters in Rochester, New York.

Donna threw herself into the job. Traveling from state to state, she would work in the field all day then stay up half the night doing paperwork. Her dedication paid off. She was soon assigned to the New York area as a sales representative. For a 23-year-old, barely out of college, it was quite a leap.

Kodak knew it had a young fireball on its hands, and in late 1980 they offered Donna a transfer to the fast-growing area of Orange County on the southern edge of Los Angeles. The new location offered tremendous potential, and Donna loved a challenge. In January of 1981, she moved to an apartment in Fullerton and went to work. Over the next year, she won numerous sales contests, and the prize that pleased her most was the trip for two to Las Vegas.

Friends and co-workers teased her about whom she would be asking to go with her. "What guy are you taking?" they wanted to know.

"I'm going with my girlfriend," she told them. "Then we can meet guys who will take us places. I want to have fun!"

More than anything, Donna wanted to show her dear friend, Barbara Arkins, the time of her life. They had been best friends in New York and this trip was a bit of bribery to entice Barbara to move to Los Angeles.

When Barbara arrived at Los Angeles International Airport, Donna was anxiously waiting to pick her up. Rather than heading directly to Las Vegas, they made their way to Mammoth Resort in the Sierra Nevada Mountains for a weekend of skiing. Early Monday morning they were on the road again, heading for Las Vegas, driving through Death Valley along the way. Once in Las Vegas they checked into the MGM Grand and made plans for the evening. Frank Sinatra was appearing at Caesar's Palace and both girls were big Sinatra fans.

As Donna and Barbara dressed for dinner and the show, my client and I were just leaving Aspen in his private 727, heading back to Los Angeles. Bob Franks was a Los Angeles multi-millionaire real estate developer whose life consisted of fun and games. Bob spotted a glow on the horizon. Ahead was Las Vegas. Suddenly he wanted to add excitement to the evening with bright lights and entertainment, so we made the decision to have dinner in Vegas.

From the Las Vegas airport, Bob and I took a limousine to the MGM Grand. We wandered first into the casino up to the "21" table. Within a matter of minutes we won $17,000.00 and special attention from the management. Although Bob and I looked like we had just spent a night camping in the mountains, we were offered dinner on the house. As we headed into the restaurant and took our VIP booth, we noticed Donna and Barbara sitting alone at the table across from us. "Good evening, ladies," Bob smiled. "May we send you a drink? Is Dom Perignon okay?"

Donna and Barbara looked at each other as if to say, "Who are these guys?" In their minds they thought these men were older, in their forties, not especially well-dressed but interesting nevertheless. Barbara replied, "That would be just fine, thank you." Then Bob asked the girls to join us for dinner and promised them a real feast. Intrigued and curious, the girls accepted the invitation and the night of fun began.

Around nine o'clock, Donna leaned over to Barbara and whispered, "We'd better tell them we have to go to Caesar's to see Sinatra's show." Then she turned to say, "Thanks for a great time but we have to go. . . ."

"I heard you say Sinatra," I interrupted. "Is Francis in town?"

"Who calls Sinatra 'Francis'?" Donna mumbled.

"He's an old friend of mine," I said. "I've known him for years. Come on, we'll have your elbows on the stage to see the show."

The girls couldn't believe their good fortune. The Dom Perignon and dinner was one thing, but knowing Frank Sinatra was something else. The distance between the MGM Grand and Caesar's Palace was only a few hundred yards, but I insisted they let us take them in a limousine. In the few minutes it took to get from the limo to the main showroom, I explained how I met Sinatra. Following a hitch in the army in 1960, I went to Los Angeles where I found employment at the famed Beverly Wilshire Hotel. Although I knew little about the hotel business, I liked what I saw and decided to learn as much as I could from the ground up. I worked hard and learned fast, and Hernando Courtright, Beverly Wilshire's legendary owner, recognized my work ethic and ability to please his guests. As the master hotelier's protégé, it wasn't long before I was appointed General Manager of the landmark Beverly Hills showplace.

It was at the Beverly Wilshire that I earned the trust and friendship of many notables—entertainers, captains of industry, political figures, coaches, such people as John F. Kennedy, Robert Kennedy, Lyndon Johnson, Richard Nixon, Gerald Ford, Ronald Reagan, George Bush, Kirk Kerkorian, Paul Bear Bryant, Ara Parseghian, John McKay, Elvis, Elizabeth Taylor and Frank Sinatra, to name a few. The success of Sinatra's gala 50th birthday party at the hotel, which I planned and orchestrated, served to cement our relationship. We continued our friendship long after I left the hotel in 1970 to pursue new challenges.

Now we sat stage-side with Donna Jones and Barbara Arkins at Caesar's Palace. When Sinatra came on stage, he acknowledged me immediately and from time to time throughout the performance, Sinatra would glance at our table, wink and grin. The ladies loved it.

The next morning, as Donna and Barbara dressed to go out for breakfast, they heard a knock on their door. A voice announced "room service," but they hadn't ordered anything. As they opened the door, a cart was wheeled in bearing two dozen roses and breakfast for two of eggs Benedict, fresh fruit, coffee—and champagne on ice! A moment later, the phone rang. "Hello, ladies," a voice said. "Enjoying your breakfast?" It was Bob. Then he added, "How would you like to see the Grand Canyon from the sky?" They didn't say no.

That day and the next were filled with non-stop excitement: plane rides, casinos, celebrity entertainment, and lavish meals. When the time came for Donna and Barbara to return to Los Angeles, I said, "Fly back with us." I even offered to call my chauffeur to Las Vegas in order to have Donna's car driven back to her apartment. Donna couldn't agree to that. The car belonged to Kodak, and she would not let anyone else drive it. That impressed me—young yet responsible.

At the end of the week, Barbara regretfully flew home to New York and Donna went back to work in Los Angeles. But Donna and I kept in touch. I think

ONE MORE SUNSET

Donna recognized an opportunity for me to help her in business, and I saw great potential for her to be extremely successful. We hit it off from the start, enjoyed each other's company and seemed to energize each other. Donna was bright and enthusiastic. She had a joyous, youthful spirit. I was in my prime as a successful businessman, financial advisor and confidant. My experience in working with people in various fields, the highs and lows of daily dealings, was most helpful to Donna in her sales position with Kodak.

Over the next few years, I took the role of being Donna's mentor and we became close friends. Because of Donna's love for travel, she accompanied me on short trips to Catalina and Aspen, longer ones to Hawaii and Tahiti, evenings with ice hockey great Wayne Gretzky and country star Larry Gatlin.

However, for all our time spent together, the relationship was not a romantic one. We enjoyed many of the same things, shared many of the same opinions. But both of us were independent, dynamic people. We led very separate lives but shared a deep mutual respect and trust.

For Donna, winning the trip to Las Vegas at the Kodak sales meeting that afternoon in 1982 was a high point in her life, opening her world to new friendships and experiences. However, the event that changed her life took place on April 8, 1985. In one swift moment, it drastically changed not only the life of Donna Jones but also my life and all who knew us well.

CHAPTER 2

Too Long on the Ice

"Why waste your vacation time?" I asked Donna. "It won't be that much fun. We're going on business." But this time it wasn't the fun but the mention of Montana that had her ready to start packing. Donna had never been to Montana and it was her goal to visit all 50 states. She had 17 to go, and she had to reach this goal before one of her brothers, Tommy, beat her to it. Donna and her brothers had an ongoing friendly competition. Donna Jones loved competition—and she loved to win.

For me, as Bob's business manager, the purpose of this trip to Montana was to prevent the real estate deal from closing. The first indication that Bob was up to something in Montana had come only a few days earlier, during the first week in April of 1985. I'd received a late night phone call from Bob to inform me that he'd purchased a lodge in the mountains of Montana. Knowing Bob as I did, I had a feeling there was more to the story than he was telling me.

Bob was a generous man, but there were always strings attached. He used his wealth primarily to draw attention to himself. He lived a purely hedonistic lifestyle, pushing buttons and pushing limits. His behavior was often outrageous. It gave him great pleasure to defy the odds in fast cars, fast boats and fast planes. To Bob, skimming the waves along the

California coast at 500 mph in his personal Saberliner was child's play.

His risk-taking extended to his business dealings as well. When he told me he had bought the lodge in Montana, skepticism was my initial reaction. I wondered if he hadn't received the extraordinary attention from the owners that he often craved which may have provoked him to buy the place. He had acquired various other holdings on impulse for the same reason. Many times before Bob had initiated a number of business deals, only to call me in at the last minute to quash them. I believed that Montana was another such adventure.

Donna overheard me discussing the business trip to Montana and she excitedly asked if she could go with us. She knew Bob wouldn't mind because they were good buddies. He enjoyed Donna's company and she was a great audience.

In my mind, this wasn't the best time for Donna to be taking a day off. After winning virtually every sales award Kodak's Whittier office had to offer at its most recent awards banquet, she'd been further rewarded with a generous bonus and a new territory that included the area's prime beach cities. Eager to live close to the ocean, she'd rented a bright, airy apartment in Manhattan Beach only days before. From her living room windows she had a full view of the ocean and breathtaking Pacific sunsets.

It was Easter weekend. Donna was in the process of moving when she heard about the trip. Her new apartment was loaded with boxes, still needing to be unpacked, but that didn't matter. She wanted to get to Montana and check another state off her "had to see" list.

On Monday morning, April 8, Donna picked me up at my beach house in Venice and we drove to LAX. Bob's plane, a custom 727 mansion in the sky, was ready to board when we arrived, decorated with fresh flowers, the sounds of Willie Nelson and champagne on ice. We greeted Bob and his girlfriend, Lori, his sisters and their husbands, and we were off. For me, it was just another business trip. For Donna, traveling in luxury and being with Bob and his family was something special. She intended to have as much fun as possible during her one-day stay in Montana.

Knowing Donna's passion for flowers, Bob suggested she take the bouquets from the plane with her to the lodge. We deplaned at Missoula airport, her arms filled with colorful blooms. She immediately wanted her picture taken. Donna always carried a camera with her. She was Kodak to the core. Her CB name was Shutterbug.

From the plane, Bob's family headed to a van for the eighty-mile drive to the lodge. The rest of us boarded a waiting helicopter. During the 20-minute flight, Bob instructed his pilot to drop low as we approached Seeley Lake. He wanted us to see where he had been snowmobiling on his previous trip. Snowmobiling was Bob's latest attempt at living on the edge. The experience had been so exhilarating for him that it was to be the focus of the day's activities. Donna looked forward to joining Bob in his newly discovered sport—snowmobiling on a frozen lake.

The scene was spectacular. It was a flawless day, calm and peaceful. The tree-covered mountains were blanketed with snow, and as the copter descended onto a clearing, the frozen lake came into view. How could we know that in just a few hours, so many lives—Donna's, mine and those of our families and friends—would not only be forever altered but shredded for years to come?

Jim and Robin Busch, the owners of the property, introduced us to the lodge manager, Roger Watson and his wife, Geri. It was easy to see why Bob was so taken with the place. The people were friendly and the lodge building was warm and inviting. Set among the trees and mountain ranges, with glorious views in all directions, the rustic, all-wood structure seemed to disappear into the surroundings. Inside were blazing fireplaces, an indoor swimming pool and steam and sauna baths.

The original agenda for the day had included a business meeting to be followed by lunch and a free afternoon. At the last minute, Bob postponed the meeting until after lunch. That plan, too, was canceled in favor of an exhibition of sharp-shooting by Jim Busch. It was becoming more and more obvious that Bob wanted to avoid talking business.

The sharp-shooting session lasted longer than anyone anticipated. At last, it was over and the sun was beginning to set. Once again, Bob postponed the meeting. It was time to go snowmobiling, he announced, assembling his group. Donna, Roger, Jennifer (Bob's niece), and five others gathered around him.

Donna had long been ready to go, dressed in her warmest winter garb with state-of-the-art equipment—a colorful leather suit and gloves and, of course, a helmet. She stood on the front porch of the lodge to show me that she was prepared to experience new thrills on the frozen lake. With a "thumbs up" sign and a big smile, she took off to join the others. In those days, Donna wore her blonde hair in a pageboy, just as June Allyson did when she played the girl-next-door in her MGM movies. I had bought Donna a photo of June Allyson at an MGM memorabilia store. She felt flattered that I likened her to a movie star.

As Donna walked away, I began to wander around the property. The sun had set and the air was turning icy, stinging my face and lungs. It was nearly 5:00 p.m. Suddenly, the quiet of late afternoon was broken by the roar of departing snowmobile engines. Somehow, it seemed, snowmobiles didn't belong in such a pristine and peaceful environment.

I returned to the warmth of the lodge where I joined Bob's sisters. It came as no surprise to hear them say they didn't care for the place, but were afraid to tell him. They were afraid they'd be saddled with the lodge once Bob inevitably lost interest in it. As we talked, I found myself assuring them that I would convince Bob not to buy the property, even though I knew he didn't need convincing.

As late afternoon turned into early evening, we settled back before the warm glow of a crackling fireplace to await the return of the snowmobilers.

Down at Seeley Lake, the atmosphere was not as calm and comfortable. Roger Watson remembered: "It was a black, black night. There were stars but no moon, and it was impossible to see anything farther away than your hand unless it had a light on it."

Roger recalled, "We'd been racing around on the frozen lake for an hour or so when I saw the lights of one snowmobile moving real fast in the distance. I knew there was open water out that way so I took off on my snowmobile, going about 65 mph to stop whoever it was. When I caught up with it I yelled to the driver to back off. When I finally got it stopped I discovered the driver was Bob Franks.

"Bob and I were talking when Rick Hawthorne, an employee of Bob's, came up and parked beside us. We turned our motors off and just shot the breeze while the others motored around on the ice. In the distance we could see the red taillights of the other snowmobiles as they headed farther down the lake. In that dark night, it was difficult to tell how far away the snowmobiles were."

With increasing emotion, Roger continued. "Only minutes later the red taillights were replaced by white headlights," he said. "Bob suggested that we start one of our snowmobiles so that the others could see us as they headed back in our direction. He fired up his machine, which automatically turned on its red taillight, then let the motor idle.

"The four snowmobiles were getting closer as they raced across the frozen surface of the lake. Then three of the headlights went suddenly dim, an indication of lowered acceleration. The fourth light, however, stayed bright. The driver apparently hadn't noticed that the others had backed off on their throttles, and so it kept on coming. And it was flying!

"I figured one of the drivers was just goofing off and would go soaring by us. But it didn't happen that way. The driver obviously misjudged the distance, for by the time we appeared in the headlights, it was too late. The machine was out of control and accelerating, as if the throttle were stuck in the open position. The driver attempted to swerve and miss us, rather than hitting the brakes. In doing so, the shags on the snowmobile's skis dug into the ice and flipped the machine, hurling it 15 feet into the air over Rick's head. On landing, the driver fell free and shot across the ice like a rocket, slamming into the back of Bob's idling snowmobile. The impact was so heavy that as the body wrapped around the machine, it moved the 500-pound snowmobile, with Bob sitting in it, six feet down the ice, tearing off its trailer hitch. The driver's body then sailed by, its head hitting me in the shin and knocking me down.

"It happened so fast," continued Roger, "so our first reaction was, 'What the hell was that?' Then we raced over to the fallen driver, who was lying face down. I rolled the body over and saw that it was Donna. With the snowmobile light focused on her, I could see her eyes were fixed and fully dilated. Turning to Bob, I said, 'My God, I think she's dead!' Bob backed away. 'No, no, she can't be,' he screamed. 'Don't say that!'"

Roger hadn't known Bob very long, but it quickly became clear that Bob was emotionally ill-equipped to deal with such emergencies. He couldn't handle such news. "He didn't want to know about Donna," said Roger. "Nothing at all. I knew then that Bob wasn't our man to help with this emergency. He just wanted to get away, and so we sent him for help. He headed toward the Goode's place, a house at the edge of the lake which had the nearest phone."

If there was any life in Donna, Roger and Rick knew they didn't have any time to waste. Minutes had passed already. "As Bob wandered away," recalled Roger, "I began giving her mouth-to-mouth resuscitation. I'd never done that before, but she wasn't breathing and I had to get air into her lungs. Her jaw was crunchy as I put my mouth to hers and sucked blood from her throat. Then solid matter began to come up, chunks of lettuce and other bits of food. The passage finally cleared and I forced air into her. But no air came out."

It was about 7:00 p.m. Back at the lodge, Roger's wife, Geri, answered the phone. When she hung up a moment later, she turned to me and said, "That was Bob. There's been an accident." Bob's sisters gathered around and we looked at each other with great concern.

"An accident? Where?" I asked.

"He didn't give any details," she answered, "but he didn't sound alarmed. All he said was to send his helicopter to the lake as soon as possible."

One by one we started asking questions. We didn't know where they were or what we should do. Could we go out there and find them?

"I don't know any more," Geri said. "He didn't give any details. He just hung up . . . rather abruptly."

"Was anybody hurt?"

"That's all I know," Geri repeated a second time. "But I doubt there's anything to worry about. Bob sounded calm, like there wasn't any urgency."

"But the helicopter. Didn't he say to get it there as soon as possible?" This was a contradiction in my mind and I was getting nervous.

Geri was back on the phone again, this time with Bob's helicopter pilot. From the look on her face she wasn't having any success getting him to fly the mountains at night. "Perhaps Bob should make other arrangements," the pilot suggested.

Fortunately, Bob called again only moments later. After relaying his pilot's message, Geri recommended calling the hospital in Missoula to request their rescue helicopter, if necessary. As before, Bob seemed to be in no hurry to push the emergency button. He did, however, admit that the injured party was one of the two girls in the group. Then he hung up again, leaving us to wonder which one of the girls was hurt.

"Well, it's 50-50 that it's either your daughter, Jennifer, or Donna," I said, turning to Bob's sister, Helen. She looked away, not knowing what to do or say. None of us did. We were all surprisingly calm, no tears or hysteria. But, then, we had so little to go on, and according to Bob, no reason to panic.

We tried to make small talk to take our minds off the disturbing news, but that didn't help. And so we sat quietly staring into space with our thoughts. My mind started racing. Was Bob purposely being noncommittal to protect us? Was the news worse than he was letting on? Which one of the girls had been involved in the accident . . . and how seriously was she injured? Was it Jennifer? Or was it Donna?

The phone rang again and Geri hurried to answer it. She mouthed "Bob" to us as she listened, then she slowly lowered the receiver. "It's Donna," she announced, finally, ". . . but he said she's okay."

ONE MORE SUNSET

I took a deep breath and jumped to my feet. "Take me out to the lake," I told Geri. "I have to see for myself what's going on." We grabbed sleeping bags, blankets, and bundled up. Then we stepped outside into the sharp night air and climbed on two parked snowmobiles. We hadn't gone very far when my machine stopped. It was so dark that I had steered into a deep slush bank. Unable to pull out of the mire, and not wanting to waste time, I hopped on the back of Geri's snowmobile. Together we made our way through the thick, black forest.

As we reached the edge of the lake, we saw some lights in the distance and headed for them. With each passing second they grew brighter until we were suddenly at the accident scene. Abandoned snowmobiles sat idling on the ice facing in various directions and a small group of people stood motionless in the red glare of taillights. No sooner did Geri bring her snowmobile to a stop than Bob Franks was at my side. "She's okay, Jimmy," he said, reassuringly, "Donna's okay."

Somewhere in the background, I could hear Geri talking to her husband. "How's she doing?" Geri asked.

"She's dying, for Christ's sake!" was Roger's gasping reply.

It was then that I saw Donna lying on the ice, spotlighted in the glare of headlights from the ring of surrounding snowmobiles. Roger was hunched over her, his mouth upon hers, intermittently blowing in, then pausing as Rick, kneeling beside her, pressed down on her chest. With her helmet still on, she looked like a broken doll, her face twisted and covered with lacerations. One of her teeth was missing. Her jaw was no longer straight and strong, but set at an odd angle. I knelt beside her and gently cupped her bloody face in my hands. Looking down at her, rage raced through my body and for a moment I felt paralyzed and completely helpless. She wasn't moving, but I could clearly hear her moans. I turned to Bob and screamed, "Is this your idea of 'okay'?" He looked at me without saying a word, then climbed on his snowmobile and sped away.

Rick and Roger pulled me back from Donna. I started roaming in circles, crying. Looking at Donna, I felt sick and weak all over. My legs nearly collapsed. Powerless, I could only turn to God, and looking up at the sky I yelled, "We need your help!"

I pleaded with someone, anyone, to tell me what had happened. Roger filled me in the best he could. Help was on the way, he promised, but how soon it would arrive was impossible to tell. Donna seemed near death. She was unable to breathe on her own for longer than a few minutes at a time. Without help, and soon, she would die. She had lost pulse twice, but was pulled back to life each time through the heroic efforts of Roger and Rick. Could she survive at all was the frightening question.

Donna desperately needed immediate medical assistance. The accident had taken place at approximately 6:30 p.m. It was now shortly after 7:30. My anger toward Bob was explosive. He let the "golden hour" pass because he was a coward and a liar.

Geri left to call 911 after dropping me off. For the next two hours, Roger, Rick and I huddled against Donna, trying to keep her warm while holding her hand, talking to her, letting her know we were there for her. We had wrapped her in blankets as best we could, but the night was bitterly cold and she was literally lying on ice. Every once in a while one of us would feel an almost imperceptible squeeze from her hand or notice her move ever so slightly, or hear her moan. They were faint signals that Donna was still alive, and that gave us hope.

Rick received word that a helicopter was on the way. Just minutes later we heard the roar of approaching snowmobiles. As the roar grew louder, I heard Roger cry out, "She's stopped breathing again!" He put his mouth to Donna's and blew air into her. Her chest rose and Rick pushed the air out.

"It's the Quick Rescue Unit," someone yelled. I stood up and joined the others in waving to the QRU, a group of local lifesavers from nearby Swan Valley. "Over here!" we shouted. "She's over here!"

"How's she doing?" shouted one of the men from the QRU as his snowmobile slowed to a stop.

Looking up from his kneeling position over Donna, Roger said, "This girl is dying."

Roger was speaking the truth, I knew, but I didn't want to hear it. I only wanted to see Donna being cared for and in the hands of people who would make her well and strong again.

The crew from the rescue unit worked feverishly over Donna, pushing tubes down her throat, hooking her up to an IV and tending to her until the helicopter could carry her away to the hospital. At one point, the man closest to Donna raised his head and said in a low voice, "This is real serious."

Word that the hospital helicopter had landed brought a sigh of relief. The news came from one of the QRU volunteers who had a radio and was now in contact with the helicopter pilot. But there was a major problem. The pilot felt the ice was too soft. He was afraid to touch down on the lake and so he had landed in a clearing several miles away.

"That's crazy!" Roger yelled. "We had a helicopter land here just two days ago. It's solid!"

The pilot wouldn't listen. Donna would have to be transported to the helicopter.

"That's too risky," countered the man with the radio, explaining that Donna would not survive the trek over the miles of rough terrain to the landing site.

But the pilot was unyielding. He would not chance moving any closer.

With no other way out, the decision was made to move Donna to the helicopter. She was gently placed on a stretcher, then lifted and secured aboard a snowmobile. As we started to move slowly ahead, Donna's vital signs again disappeared—no pulse, no breathing. She wouldn't be able to make it, the rescue team determined, so they stopped the snowmobile and set her back down on the ice.

"God help her!" I cried. It was a prayer, a plea, a command. Something had to be done to save her, but nothing was going right.

As Donna lay unconscious with the rescue team furiously trying to revive her, Rick suddenly took off on a snowmobile. He soon returned with the pilot to prove to him the ice was safe by core-holing into it. When the plug was removed, its thickness was enough evidence for the pilot. As Rick sped the pilot back to the helicopter, Roger shouted, "If you don't make it back with the helicopter, she'll die!"

He did come back. We heard a whirring sound above the trees, growing stronger as a beacon of light came steadily toward us. The helicopter hovered over the ice, blowing clouds of powdery snow in our faces, as it slowly lowered to within inches of the frozen surface. The pilot set it down ever so gently.

The arrival of the helicopter seemed to take place in slow motion. Once it landed, however, everything speeded up. Donna, still on the stretcher, was quickly lifted on board. I attempted to climb in too, but the pilot informed me he had taken the seat out to accommodate the stretcher and there was no room for me. Then the doors slammed shut and we all backed away.

We were so relieved that Donna would finally be on her way to the hospital. Crying with emotional exhaustion, we waved and cheered at her departure.

It was an eerie ovation. Donna was barely clinging to life. There were no guarantees that she would even get to the hospital in time. There were no guarantees that she could be saved once she got there.

The churning blades of the departing helicopter created a deafening roar, followed by a blinding wind, a tornado of swirling ice and snow. The helicopter lifted higher and higher, then faded into the darkness. Donna was on her way at last! I raised my arms in thankfulness and hopeful celebration. What an exit, I told myself—the drama, the commotion, the spectacle. I looked up into the sky and said in a soft voice, "Donna would have loved it."

CHAPTER 3

Diagnosis: Traumatic Closed Head Injury

How long I had stared at the departing helicopter, I don't know. I can only remember looking up into the black sky, seeing only pinpoints of light from the millions of faraway stars and feeling an over-whelming sadness and helplessness that I had felt only once before in my life. I drifted into the past, reliving the moment when I stood at the bedside of my 10-year-old niece, Luanne, as she lay unconscious in a hospital twenty years earlier. She had contracted measles and then encephalitis. She developed a very high fever and fell into a deep coma. I remembered standing over her small, motionless body in the emergency room, feeling completely powerless as the doctor explained to us there was a possibility Luanne may not wake up.

I snapped back to the present and thoughts of Donna as I felt a hand on my arm. "Come on!" Rick said anxiously, waving for me to climb aboard one of the idling snowmobiles. "We've got to get moving." We quickly headed back to the lodge where we borrowed a truck for the long ride to Missoula.

Three hours had passed since Donna was injured. It took us an additional two hours to make the grueling drive to the hospital. That journey to St. Patrick's Hospital in Missoula seemed to take forever, as we rode along a rough and winding snow-covered road, staring blankly at the high beam of our headlights. During that time, Rick and I sat mostly in silence, each with our own thoughts. I was numb from the cold and I kept wondering if Donna were still alive. The sight of her limp body lying in the snow flashed in and out of my mind. I could see Donna's face, then Luanne's face. I kept hearing the chilling voices of Roger and the crew of the rescue unit as they worked so desperately to revive Donna.

As time dragged on, I became more apprehensive. I pledged to myself that if Donna survived I would do everything humanly possible to make her well again.

It was past midnight when we pulled into the driveway of the hospital's emergency area. The waiting room was empty except for the woman standing behind the desk. "We're here about Donna Jones," I said, the words hurriedly tumbling out. "She was brought in by helicopter."

The woman nodded without expression.

"How is she doing?" I asked, anxiously.

"What is your relationship to Miss Jones?" she wanted to know. I'd been in hospitals before and there was no way I was going to find out anything unless I was related to Donna. "I'm her brother Jimmy," I lied.

The woman offered no information other than Donna was in surgery. But that was enough. Donna was still alive!

Rick and I looked at each other as if to say, "Thank God." Then we sat down and waited. But every time the phone rang, my heart jumped. I couldn't stand it, so I took a walk. After about fifteen minutes I came back. It wasn't much later when a man dressed in soiled hospital whites came out to meet us. He looked exhausted, and he was carrying something in his hand along with what appeared to be Donna's snow boots.

"I'm Dr. Roth," he said simply. "These are Donna's." He held out the snow boots and I took them.

Then he handed me Donna's diamond earrings and Rolex watch. "That's all we could save," he added. "Her clothing had to be cut off when she was brought in." Pleadingly, I looked into the doctor's eyes, fearing the worst.

"She's still alive," he said solemnly. "Believe me, if she could live through the operation, and she has, there's a chance she can make it. She's in great physical condition, and that has helped her so far."

"What about the surgery?" Rick asked. Dr. Roth led us over to the waiting room chairs and we all sat down.

He was a gentle and caring man as he outlined the extent of Donna's injuries. They were even more extensive than I had imagined.

"When Donna was brought in," he said, "she had a lot of bleeding in her stomach. We found a laceration of her liver, and I operated on that. She also had a collapsed lung and some other things that were more of a minor nature . . . a broken jaw that we fixed, damage to one of the bones in her hand, a tooth missing, some rib damage."

"How many ribs were broken?" I asked. It seemed like a good question at the time but Dr. Roth quickly put it in perspective.

"Those ribs won't make the difference. Donna has a much more serious problem than that. She's suffered a brain injury and remains unconscious."

"A brain injury?" I repeated.

Dr. Roth took a deep breath and went on. "We put it in the category of a closed head injury. There wasn't a big clot or anything in there that needed taking out but, remember, Donna came close to dying several times. She still had a heartbeat, but when blood pressure is so low you can't feel a pulse, you're coming very close to death. And with extremely low blood pressure for a period of time, the brain doesn't receive enough blood. That's what happened to Donna. She had extremely low blood pressure for hours before she was brought in—and it only takes a few minutes of not having a good flow to the brain to cause damage. In other words, if the person isn't taken care of immediately, chances are there will be a problem. At this point, however, it's really too early to tell how much damage has been done. We'll be monitoring her closely overnight." He paused momentarily, then added, "I suggest you come back in the morning. We'll know more then." With a faint smile, Dr. Roth reached out to shake our hands. "I'm sorry I don't have better news," he said, sympathetically, "but we'll do all we can for her . . . and she is still alive."

I must have been in a state of shock as Rick and I walked across the street to the local hotel. I was numb. I couldn't feel anything. Once in my room, I collapsed from exhaustion, sleeping all night in my clothes.

At 7:00 a.m. the next morning we walked back to the hospital. I couldn't wait to see Donna. The doctor's words had somehow become a faraway memory. In my mind, I pictured Donna as alert and well, sitting up and smiling her big smile as she waited for me to take her home. Instead, I was confronted with brutal reality.

As I walked into her room in the intensive care unit, I saw Donna for the first time since she'd been carried away from Seeley Lake. She was lying motionless in the bed, virtually lifeless, surrounded by beeping machines and stainless steel poles holding clear bags of liquids. Tubes sprouted from every part of her body, like ropes on an oversized marionette. Her face, head and neck were discolored and swollen. Two prongs fed her nostrils with oxygen. For a split-second, I didn't know whether to reach out or back away. I was overcome with agony and despair.

I moved toward her and stroked her head gently. "You're going to be okay," I said softly to her. I could barely find my voice.

A second meeting with Donna's surgeon, Dr. Roth, didn't bring the positive news I was hoping to hear. Donna had indeed suffered a major head injury and was in deep trouble. "Her brain has swollen and shut everything else down," Dr. Roth said. "We'll have to be patient until the swelling subsides. Once that happens we'll be able to determine the real consequences of her injury. But experience tells us that if she wakes up within 6 days, she'll have a very good chance of recovery." The doctor turned to leave and we said good-bye.

Alone again with Donna, I stood at her bedside staring into space, unable to fully comprehend, maybe even refusing to believe, that a tragedy of such enormity had befallen this wonderful young woman. Only hours earlier she had been so animated, so vital, so alive; her future held such promise. Now she was struggling to stay alive. She had beaten the odds so far and I desperately wanted to believe she had the courage and strength to live.

Since we met, Donna had looked to me for guidance when things appeared insurmountable, but this was unfamiliar territory for me. I had no experience and I felt so completely helpless. If Donna were going to recover, she would need help from someone much more powerful than I.

For the next three hours, I sat at Donna's side, praying for a miracle, holding her hand and searching her face for some indication of life. I begged her to squeeze my hand or open her eyes, anything to let me know that she was aware of my presence. It was selfish of me, in a way, for I knew that the time had come to notify Donna's mother, and I wanted to be able to give her some positive news.

Reluctantly leaving Donna, I met with the hospital officials to admit that I was not Donna's brother but rather a good friend. Then I asked for their assistance in making the call to Donna's mother, Jean, wanting to have knowledgeable backup in case she asked questions I couldn't answer. We moved to a phone in a private office and placed the call to the bank in New Haven, Connecticut, where Jean was employed. I was concerned about Jean so I spoke with Jean's manager first, explaining Donna's terrible accident to her. She then called Jean into her office, away from customers.

How do you tell a mother that her daughter has been tragically injured and lies in a coma nearly a continent away? There are no easy words. With tears streaming down my face and a cracking voice, I started, but never finished. A lovely lady from Pastoral Care, those dedicated, gentle people who provide counseling for those in distress, eventually took the phone from me and finished the story. I spoke to Jean again and told her it was important for her to come to Montana immediately. "I'll make all the arrangements," I said, and she agreed to take the next possible flight. I then called my secretary in Los Angeles and asked her to make the arrangements for Jean.

There were other important calls to make as well. I contacted my sister, Angela, in Los Angeles who, in turn, called our mother, Clare. Angela promised they would join me in Montana as soon as possible.

I then called Roy and Betty Noble in Los Angeles, who were longtime, cherished friends. I first met Roy 15 years earlier at the Marina City Club where I had my office. I had complete trust in him, like a brother. His wife, Betty, had worked at Daniel Freeman Hospital in Inglewood as a registered nurse since 1959.

Following the phone calls, I returned to the intensive care unit. There had been no change in Donna's condition.

It was now evening, almost 24 hours after the accident, and I met Donna's mother at the airport. A small, thin woman, she appeared to be on the verge of collapse. With nothing to do but wonder and worry across the miles, the long flight had taken its toll on her.

On our way to the hospital I tried to prepare Jean as best I could. I told her about Donna being unconscious and about the tubes, as well as facial cuts. But, nothing can truly prepare a mother to see her child lying in a coma, battered and bruised and hooked up to wires, tubes, and beeping monitors.

Over the next few minutes, I watched the tearful meeting of a heartbroken mother and her tragically wounded daughter. Moments of reaching out without response, moments of deadly silence. Jean and Donna had been so close. Even after Donna's transfer to the West Coast they had remained in constant touch. Now they were unable to communicate with each other.

I'd thought that Jean would stay in the motel only a block from the hospital. But after seeing her with her daughter I felt it was important for them to be together that first night, and arrangements were made for Jean to sleep at the hospital. She would check into the motel the next day.

Bob Franks and his family paid an unexpected visit later that evening. They wanted to check on Donna's condition and meet Jean before returning to Los Angeles. Bob was getting ready for a trip to France; he was to leave within a few days. Taking me aside, he remarked, "I have every confidence in your ability to handle this situation on your own." Then he lowered his voice and added, "I honestly feel you are far more competent in these situations than I am." With that, and a pat on the back, he was gone.

Within the week, my family and friends began to arrive to offer their support and assist with Donna's care. It was a relief to see familiar faces again, and to know that Donna's chance of awakening to the sight of a friendly face was greatly enhanced. Until their arrival, my schedule had been set in stone: 15 minutes at Donna's bedside, five minutes in the church behind the hospital, and 40 minutes in the local bar. Then I'd return to her bedside, talk to her, try to wake her up, and touch her to let her know I was there.

Roy and Betty Noble were the first to arrive. Seeing Donna for the first time was a shock to everyone. As Betty remembered, "It was heartbreaking to see her like that. She had always been such a vivacious person, and then to see her lying so still. I've worked with people in comas, but when it's someone you know, a family member or a close friend, your feelings are different. Not that you don't always have empathy for the patients and families. But with Donna, it was quite different. She was a special friend."

Betty and Roy were tireless in their devoted attention to Donna, speaking to her, constantly rubbing or caressing her arms and hands in an effort to break through to her subconscious. Words, sounds and touch were so important. Somehow, Donna had to be made aware that she was not alone, that we were there for her.

On April 11, three days after the accident, my mother and sister arrived. We began to have the makings of a great team surrounding Donna. But it was not without sacrifice. Roy and Betty had to temporarily leave their jobs to come to Missoula. My mother, Clare, who owned and operated a successful business in Marina Del Rey, also closed shop for a while.

On my mother's first night in Montana, neither of us went to bed. I was emotionally out of control. Between crying and drinking, I tried to describe the details of the accident to her. My mother sat there listening, crying too. We were both overcome with grief and disbelief.

I knew the trip would be hard on everyone, but it was Angela who most concerned me. She was a single parent with four children and I had always pitched in whenever possible, earning the nickname of "bachelor father." But there was little I could do when her daughter,

Luanne, caught the measles and developed encephalitis, dying in 1965. She was just ten at the time, and would have been Donna's age had she lived. I was afraid Angela would relive the tragedy of her own daughter's dying when she saw Donna in a coma.

The day after her arrival in Montana, Angela came to the hospital carrying a package. She had heard a therapist mention that people who are in comas, or bedridden for a time, often develop "heel drop," a condition that has their toes curling up from lack of use. "I told the therapist I had an idea," Angela said, " and the therapist approved. So I went out and bought Donna a pair of blue high-top Reeboks." Those little shoes looked so cheerful on Donna, and they seemed to help—at least that's what everyone told me. Angela had originally wanted to buy red Reeboks. Red was Donna's favorite color, but Jean said no to red. She thought red would make her look like a clown. Angela didn't argue.

Although Donna remained in a coma, we still had hope. Exactly one week after the accident, one of Donna's eyelids fluttered. The movement lasted only a split-second, but we cheered and celebrated as if it were a Super Bowl victory. The nurses, more cautious and knowledgeable about head trauma injuries, didn't share our optimism. But to us, it was a good sign and our spirits would not be dampened. We told everyone about Donna's "progress." The employees and guests at our motel were all deeply concerned about her condition and it was indeed gratifying to finally be able to say something positive. The good news and the smiles upon hearing it were much needed nourishment for my soul.

I wasted no time in thanking God for what we all considered a minor miracle. I had become obsessive about my daily visits to the chapel. Although I had gained a reputation throughout my life as being "Mr.

Fix-it," I was deeply aware who the real "Mr. Fix-it" was and how much help Donna needed in surmounting the challenges of her life. I prayed, begged, pleaded, even cried for help—usually aloud, for I was alone at the altar. I never gave a thought as to how I sounded or if anyone else was in listening range. My mind was too absorbed in sending out a prayerful message for help.

Donna's fluttering eyelid had given us such hope that as we took turns sitting with her, we were no longer just keeping her company or holding her hand. Now, we watched her motionless form intently, fearing we might miss a new sign of life.

One morning, ten days after the accident, Clare was at Donna's bedside holding her hand, when she said in a gentle voice, "Donna, it's Clare. If you hear me, press my hand." Donna did. Clare flew out of the room to locate me in the hall. She carried with her news of the first real sign that Donna "was there." Clare had tears in her eyes and halfway down the hall, she cried, "She's home!"

I ran to meet my mom and hugged her. Then I ran into Donna's room.

More signs followed. Within the next few days, Donna started to move her arms and legs, and show facial expressions. She'd been in excellent physical condition and was no stranger to exercising. Most of her leg motion seemed as if she were riding a bicycle, pumping the pedals. Although she remained in a coma, she became so active that she required restraints. One of her male nurses had served in Vietnam. Working with Donna, and trying to control her, was like being back on the battlefield, he said.

We were encouraged to see the changes in Donna's condition. Jean did not seem to be faring as well. She was becoming more and more distraught, admitting to being lonely and anxious to return to

Connecticut. What I didn't know until I met privately with Dr. Roth was that Jean intended to take Donna with her. The doctor told me that he was not supportive of Jean's decision. I responded, "What if I don't provide the funds?" Dr. Roth placed his hand on my shoulder and said, "Jim, I honestly think she'll put her on a Greyhound bus." The request had already been made to transfer Donna to Yale-New Haven Hospital, which was close to the Jones' home. While I respected Jean's wishes, I certainly did not agree with them. Donna was receiving excellent care at St. Patrick's. The hospital and staff had made Donna their special project, displaying a spirit, enthusiasm and fondness for Donna that was quite unique. She was making progress, and the entire community seemed concerned and interested in her recovery. Even the rescue helicopter pilot, whose general policy had been never to follow up on those patients whom he had transported, made an exception in Donna's case by personally visiting and monitoring her progress. I truly felt it would be more beneficial for Donna, especially in her still guarded condition, to remain in Missoula. To confirm my beliefs, I consulted with doctors not only at St. Patrick's but also at UCLA Medical Center in Los Angeles, one of the most respected facilities in the nation. I was repeatedly told that it would be best to leave Donna where she was, and that a cross-country move could prove disastrous to her.

According to Dr. Roth, I was fighting a losing battle. "We have to listen to her mother," he said, "because, well, simply, she's her mother."

I let go. I had no control. The best I could do was to help prepare Donna for the trip to Connecticut.

It was now three weeks since the accident. To help her gain some mobility, we turned her room into a giant playpen. The walls were padded with mats and all objects were moved out of reach. Her IV and catheter were removed for this short session and she was then put on the floor where she could move around without restraints. She wasn't awake. Yet she wasn't asleep.

"It's often not safe to turn patients loose when waking up from a neurological problem," said Dr. Roth. "They are often disoriented and unpredictable so restraints are often used. You never know how they're going to react. Some become even more agitated. We've had some success by getting them down on the floor where they can't fall. There's no other place to go. We simply leave them alone on the mats."

I didn't want Donna to be alone, or to feel that she was alone, so I got down on the mats with her. She behaved like a bear cub coming out of hibernation. Although her eyes were closed, she began to crawl all over me, first touching, then rubbing and sniffing my hair and body. Initially, we were told she had lost her sense of smell. Maybe she had and was only trying to smell something.

Only moments into the exercise, Jean appeared in the doorway to Donna's room. She stood silently watching as her daughter crawled over me, exploring the curves and angles of my body with her fingertips and nostrils. Then Jean quietly remarked, "I guess you really do love her." I turned to look her way and she was gone. What prompted the comment, I don't know, and I never asked. I wanted to stay focused on the moment, which was to help Donna wake up, and to begin our journey to her full recovery.

What a remarkable experience it was to observe someone in a coma attempting to connect with the outside world through touch and smell. And to be a part of it! We had been desperately looking for any signs and so, on this special day, we were elated.

The "playpen" therapy was repeated over the next several days. With each session, Donna grew less agitated and feisty. She was beginning to relax. At this point, we knew that her arms and legs were functioning well. And she was now getting nourishment through her mouth; although her jaws were wired shut, a tube was inserted through the open space created by her missing tooth. Her only other daily activity was a sponge bath. That left hours of quiet time to sit and watch and hope and pray. We needed to remind ourselves that life by the inch is a cinch. We were searching and hoping for minor miracles, and doing our best to make Donna comfortable as we waited. In our hearts, we felt certain that she would one day soon open her eyes and smile. As slowly as it seemed at times, she was making progress, and I was determined to help her keep up the momentum.

The time was coming, however, when I knew that I'd have to let go. Jean, in her way, was as determined as I was in mine. And she held the trump card. She had absolutely made up her mind to take Donna back to Connecticut with her. There was nothing I could say or do to stop her.

Reluctantly, I agreed to provide what was necessary to accomplish the complicated feat of safely transporting Donna across the country. After arranging with a hospital-aircraft company to furnish a plane, I talked with the floor nurse responsible for Donna's primary care at St. Pat's. Because she was aware of Donna's precarious condition and knew the intensity of care required, she agreed to assist during the flight.

Donna's need for special attention would surely be tested. She was still hooked up to a battery of tubes with oxygen to keep her lungs inflated, and an IV for medications. Moving her on and off the plane, not to mention the flight itself, could create enormous stress and discomfort for her.

The chartered hospital plane was to arrive on Thursday morning, May 2. After hearing the doctor's opinion about moving her, I was so distressed, knowing the risks involved in moving a patient in her condition, I couldn't watch as she was being prepared for the trip. So I spent a few quiet moments with Donna the night before and said good-bye.

The anxiety and frustration that gnawed at my insides might have lessened had she been able to respond to me. But she remained in her deep, deep sleep. I only hoped that on some level I was getting through to her. As I turned to look back at Donna one last time, I prayed for her safe journey.

CHAPTER 4

Tearful Good-byes

Donna and I were heading in opposite directions. Once she was in the air, making her way to Connecticut, I boarded a flight back to Los Angeles. I was a lousy seatmate to some poor stranger, constantly fidgeting, looking at my watch. A couple of drinks didn't help. Jean had me promise to keep in touch. I would have anyway. More than anything, I wanted access to a telephone. I had to know that Donna had arrived safely and was resting comfortably.

Early the next morning I received a call from Jean. She was crying. One of Donna's lungs had collapsed during the flight. "What did you expect?" I replied, unsympathetically. "You're lucky only a lung collapsed!"

I waited for a response, but heard only silence. Finally, she said, "I'm sorry. I never should have moved her."

I really wasn't trying to be hard on Jean, but I had to say what was on my mind. If a collapsed lung was the only setback, I told myself, then we were lucky. A collapsed lung was not life-threatening. Nevertheless, it was something else to worry about—and I was angry. Why I didn't fall to pieces then and there, I don't know.

As it turned out, the lung had no real bearing on Donna's condition and, within a few days, she was breathing comfortably again. Still, I could not shake an overwhelming anxiety. I had a vision of Donna waking up in her hospital room, coming out of her coma at last, with no one there to tell her where she was or what had happened. Alone, how would she know that she was loved, that we truly cared about her? Obsessed with this notion, and feeling helpless to gain control, I became relentless in an attempt to obtain information from Yale-New Haven Hospital.

My initial calls were directly to Donna's room. No one picked up the phone, heightening my fears. Calls followed on the hour to hospital administration, nurses, and Donna's family. Pushing for information, but unable to get enough to calm me, I hired round-the-clock nurses to be at Donna's side. To my frantic mind, someone *had* to be with Donna every second of the day and night.

Even with that program in place, I could not relax. Too many times when I called Donna's room, the phone kept ringing. Either the paid nurses I hired were busy or not present when I tried to get through. So my fears of Donna awakening to find herself alone, confused and frightened, like a child terrified by a nightmare, became unbearable. Someone had to be with her when she came out of her dark tunnel. I had to be with her.

I began flying to Connecticut twice a week, unannounced, to be at her bedside. Over the next weeks, my itinerary became routine: go to the airport without luggage, park the car, buy a ticket, board an American Airlines flight to New York, change planes there and catch another flight to Connecticut. Once in New Haven, I stayed at Donna's side. The next day found me flying back to Los Angeles. The stolen moments I spent with Donna were the only medicine that had any effect on me. It worked wonders—for a few days anyway. Then it was time to make the trip once again.

So bizarre was my ritual that I was soon on a first-name basis with the airline crew and the bartenders at JFK. There was also a bit of superstition involved. I routinely hired the same cab driver to take me to the hospital, and I checked into the same hotel room in New Haven. The pattern was strangely comforting. Aside from the nurses on duty, none of the medical staff, Donna's doctors or family members were there at the same time I was.

During one of my clandestine visits, my sister Angela joined me, arriving by train after a visit to Washington, D.C. That evening, after securing Donna for the night, Angela and I dined at a nearby restaurant. Over dinner she told me that on her arrival at the hospital she stood unobserved in the doorway to Donna's room, watching me as I cared for Donna. It had been many years since I had helped Angela raise her four children. Now, as we sat across from each other, drawing strength from each other, she admitted to thinking she would never again see that tender side of me. I had to admit that I didn't either as it had been many years since I had helped Angela raise her four children. My life had changed so much, and raising and nurturing children was a thing of the past. But a part of me, long buried, had resurfaced.

Once back in Los Angeles, much of my time was spent hauling Donna's belongings from her old apartment in Fullerton to her new apartment in Manhattan Beach. Her move to the beach the weekend before the accident had never really been completed. She had left some furniture behind in her condo and there were still lots of miscellaneous items in her cabinets to be packed. Who knew what was important, which items she needed and those she could live without? So many things, closets and cupboards filled with clothing, dishes, linens, photos and other memorabilia. If she had been there, she would have said, "Toss this. . . keep that." But she wasn't. And there was no guarantee she would ever see any of her things again.

Packing wasn't all that needed to be done. There were new utilities to be hooked up and old ones to be shut down. Her bills had to be paid and her company car returned. Once again I called on my friend Roy Noble to help me. Roy was a master at moving and organizing and we completed the list in just a few days, right before I hopped a plane back to Connecticut.

During my next visit with Donna, I asked Jean if Donna was on any medication and she told me she didn't think so, but wasn't sure. Later that day I scanned Donna's chart and discovered that she was being given three different types of medication. Having had members of my own family hospitalized over the years, I learned to monitor as closely as possible every aspect of care that is given and not to blindly accept routine procedures or activities. More importantly, I learned always to be aggressive in my approach to caring for the people I love and to seek out the most positive members of the hospital team.

It was clear that my visits and phone calls were not nearly enough to monitor Donna's situation on my own. I needed backup to help keep an eye on Donna whenever I was unable to be with her. With that in mind, I put my own CIA—Connelly's Intelligence Agency—into operation. As luck would have it, I had dear friends in the area who agreed to work with me.

Alice Fiondella, a sweet, wonderful friend from California, just happened to be in Connecticut on a prolonged visit with her family. Another dear friend from Connecticut, Alice Anderson, lived not too far from the hospital.

There was another important person in Connecticut named Nancy Clement. Nancy and Donna had been friends since fifth grade, and cheerleaders together in high school. When I arrived one day on one of my unannounced visits, Nancy was at Donna's bedside. When I saw the compassion in Nancy's eyes, I knew we had an invaluable ally. In talking with Nancy, I learned that she was a therapist, working with challenged individuals.

These three wonderful people, the two Alices and Nancy, along with members of their families, one of whom happened to be a nurse at the hospital, visited Donna regularly and reported to me in California every few days. That information, along with my continuing phone calls, provided me with a clearer picture of what was taking place with Donna at Yale-New Haven. However, I wasn't always happy with what I was hearing.

It was my perception that the doctors and hospital staff at Yale-New Haven had basically written Donna off. Yes, she had a very serious head injury and was in a coma, but the general attitude appeared to be that there was little hope for her recovery. In other words, she was history. Never did I sense a spirit of urgency or encouragement. The care she was receiving seemed impersonal and disconnected. Missing was the positive element of a team working together for her recovery.

Granted, the signs of improvement in Donna's condition were few, yet I was full of optimism, never missing an opportunity to tell anyone who would even half-listen that she was unique and special. "You'll see for yourself when she wakes up," I promised. The words were repeated over and over again: "Donna will get better. Donna will make it back. Donna is a fighter. Donna will not quit!"

I was met with blank stares, half smiles and silence—no responses, no comments, no encouragement. The on—going apathy made me more determined than ever to show them all that Donna was indeed different. I would not entertain failure.

As the days passed without reassuring news, I had to remind myself to keep thinking in a positive way. Then, on May 26, forty-eight days after the accident, I received a call from Donna's doctor that she was "beginning to communicate in the most primitive way." At first I didn't fully understand, but the point was soon made clear. Donna was coming out of her coma. She was trying to speak. The nurses reported that she was saying what sounded like my name. I jumped on the first available flight to Connecticut to celebrate the awakening.

Throughout the long plane ride I kept hearing Donna's voice in my head as she called for me. Since 1982, when we first met, we had spent a lot of time together. I had become her mentor, the one person she had always turned to for guidance and help. Was she calling for help now? If so, I wanted to let her know I was on my way.

Once I reached the hospital there was no holding me back. My emotions were beginning to overwhelm me. Mostly, I was filled with joy. Donna was awake. It was going to be just as my mother had said 48 days earlier at St. Patrick's Hospital in Missoula: "If she wakes up, she will make it. She's a fighter. She loves life."

Although it had been less than a week since I had last seen Donna, I was not prepared for the sight of her. Earlier, she had been lying down and at least looked comfortable. Now she was propped up in bed, looking so frail, so helpless and childlike, unable to hold up her head or communicate in any intelligible way. The sounds she made, the words she tried to form, were simply gibberish. A nurse told me she weighed 94 pounds and needed full-time assistance in every way.

Jean was remarkable with her. She had taken a leave of absence from the bank at the time of the accident, and although she had returned to work on a part-time basis, she was at Donna's bedside every day giving love and encouragement. Now that the wires had been removed from Donna's jaws, Jean sat patiently talking to her, stroking her, attempting to feed her. Donna's grandfather was a frequent visitor, too. He was a special favorite of Donna's and he gave her not only love but constant attention. He called her his million-dollar baby.

Donna's therapy began with her sitting in a high-backed wheelchair, her head strapped to the backboard to keep it from flopping over. She was even given her meals, which consisted of cream cereals, high protein drinks, some soups, and applesauce, while sitting in the chair. In time, we all took turns feeding her, since she was unable to do it herself. She was so weak and uncoordinated it was almost impossible for her to get or to keep food on a spoon. The few times she tried she was unable to direct it to her mouth, instead hitting the side of her face, close to her ear. And it took every ounce of strength she had.

On my second visit following Donna's emergence from her coma, I found her asleep in bed. I waited until she woke up, then helped a nurse assist her to a sitting position with her legs dangling over the side of the bed. The plan was to get Donna standing to see if she could begin supervised walking. The nurse and I helped her to stand, but after only several steps, Donna began to convulse. She began moaning and slurring and thrashing. I felt sick to my stomach. Her eyes rolled back in her head and she shook uncontrollably. The shaking lasted only seconds, but it was a terrifying few seconds. Donna had experienced a seizure. To prevent further attacks, she was given the drug Dilantin. No mention was made of possible side effects.

Seeing Donna in seizure was frightening, but what really lingered in my mind was the look of fear and concern on the nurses' faces. I wondered if Donna was really ready for physical therapy and if these nurses were qualified and prepared to handle such emergencies.

The hospital had started constructing a room for physical therapy prior to Donna's admittance. A portion of it was completed and Donna was sent there for daily therapy. On this trip to Connecticut, I left nothing to chance. As the therapist wheeled Donna down the hallway, I followed, often hiding behind large pillars, to observe not only her medical treatment but also evaluating the quality of her care. I had to know firsthand what was taking place. The sessions didn't last long. Her physical therapy consisted of lying over a large inflated ball and trying to maneuver and balance. This therapy lasted about twenty minutes, then Donna was returned to her room to sleep. She was exhausted.

After witnessing Donna's typical day, I concluded that the hospital was not adequately equipped to rehabilitate patients with head injuries. That prompted me to put Connelly's Intelligence Agency in high gear. The purpose now was much more than to "observe and report." It was to visit Donna as often as possible, thus keeping her awake and talking in order to stimulate her brain.

With all the energy created by family, friends and round-the-clock nurses, Donna was slowly beginning to respond to all the attention that she was receiving, and I truly believed we were moving in the right direction. Although her speech was badly slurred, often garbled and nonsensical, I could tell she was truly attempting to communicate with us through words. And she was on her feet, standing and moving around, although with considerable assistance.

My sister Angela spotted me one day while I was trying to help Donna learn how to walk again. I would wrap my arms tightly around her, holding her up, while her arms and legs hung limply. Angela said Donna looked so helpless, like a floppy Raggedy Ann doll. She also said I looked possessed, my eyes fixed and determined. I wouldn't give up. I'd take one step, gently nudging Donna's leg out. Then I'd take another step. It was slow, painful and tedious, but I wanted her to feel movement, rhythm. We would last about ten minutes, then we both would have to rest.

Donna had now been at Yale-New Haven for about six weeks. I tried to get to the hospital at least twice a week. In most cases, I was in and out the same day. When I wasn't with Donna, I'd talk to her by phone a minimum of six times a day. Because the accident had left her confused and with a short-term memory deficit, her response to each of my calls was always the same, full of enthusiasm and thinking I was calling for the first time. That didn't concern me because I was at least getting a response and working her brain. I made certain that Donna received phone calls all day long from as many people as possible.

In Los Angeles, I was constantly being asked about Donna's condition. Friends, neighbors and business contacts were concerned about her. My response was to tell them that she was awake and to call her in Connecticut. They did, then reported back to me about their upbeat conversations with her. What they didn't realize was Donna wouldn't remember having talked to any of them.

A simple phone call may not carry much weight with the medical world, but I honestly believed that the constant calls Donna received, along with cards and letters and prayers, became valuable therapy for her early on. What better way to let her know that everyone was pulling for her to get better? The show of support was tremendous. Positive energy flowed in Donna's direction and it was constantly working her brain.

In February of 1985, several months before the accident, Donna and I had the opportunity to attend the National Hockey League All-Star game in Calgary as guests of Wayne Gretzky. After the game we were invited to a cocktail party attended by the all-stars and other NHL players. Donna was her usual happy self and she enjoyed meeting Wayne and Larry Gatlin, who sang the national anthem prior to the game.

Following Donna's accident, both Wayne and Larry wanted to know how they could help. With Donna's 30th birthday only weeks away, this seemed like the perfect time to bring them into the picture. Two and one-half months after the accident, on the morning of June 21, Donna's big day, Wayne called her at the hospital to wish her happy birthday and offer encouragement. "Fight back and don't give up," he said. Then Larry called and sang "Happy Birthday" to her. He followed with more phone calls and a note that read: "Stay off those things (snowmobiles), darlin'. They're dangerous!"

Donna's birthday turned into an event. Her room was filled with balloons, cards and flowers. We even had to keep the switchboard operator on overtime to route all her birthday phone calls. When the cake arrived, Donna had to count the glowing candles on top. After counting 30, she announced to everyone's amazement that she was only 28. "This cake isn't for me," she said. "It's for someone else."

"It's all for you, Donna," I replied. "Today's your 30th birthday."

She smiled, shook her head emphatically and said we were all wrong. In her mind, she was only 28, and that was that!

A smile was really all Donna could manage. She had tried to laugh many times, but no sound came out. Each day was a new revelation of the changes that had taken place as a result of the accident.

We kept a radio on in her room at all times to feed sounds and information to her brain. The music meant nothing at first. But when songs from her past were played, she attempted to sing along with them. She also tried to snap her fingers to the rhythm of upbeat tunes, which she had always done prior to her injury. Now her lack of coordination made that impossible. She was unable to match up her thumb and middle finger, let alone put them together to create a snapping sound. Essentially, her fine motor skills were nonexistent.

Despite Donna's confusion with her age, the birthday celebration was a huge success. When it was over, and I told her I had to return to California, she asked to go with me. As much as it hurt to say no, I took her request as a positive sign, believing that she was becoming more aware of the world around her. It hadn't been that long ago that she was oblivious to my comings and goings. Now she was conscious of the times I was away.

"Please take me with you," she pleaded. "I won't be gone long," I told her. "Besides, you're doing just fine and it's important for you to be near your family." She started to cry, holding onto me. "Please. . . please," she sobbed. "Don't leave me here."

I didn't know what to do. She was breaking my heart and I was breaking hers. In desperation, I tried a diversionary tactic. I told her she had to stay in the hospital to take her vitamins.

She stopped crying momentarily and looked up at me. With tears in her eyes, she said simply and astonishingly, "But surely I can take them in California."

Leaving Donna was not easy, but I had no other choice. I felt like I was abandoning my child. Donna was unable to help herself, and she was at the mercy of people who were just doing a job—no more. Knowing that and seeing the hurt in her eyes, I usually ended up crying too, as I pulled away from her and headed for the door.

I was back in Los Angeles only hours when I heard from Bob Franks. Since the accident, I had limited my time and my relationship with Bob. I was no longer his hell-raising, partying business partner. It was all business on my part now, while Bob continued on his merry way.

Bob's phone call had nothing to do with his multiple properties and investments or the time I had been spending away from managing his empire. Bob simply wanted to "get away from it all" for a few days, this time to Europe, and he invited me to go with him. I proposed that *he* go to Europe and, on the way, *we* stop in Connecticut to visit Donna. He agreed, even said it was a good plan. The next evening Bob, his friend Mike Anderson and I were aboard Bob's private jet heading east. Along the way I filled everyone in on Donna's improving condition, which was enough reason for Bob to break out the champagne. He was always looking for a reason to party.

The plane landed at Tweed-New Haven Airport at 7:00 a.m. My cab was waiting, as usual, and we arrived at the hospital, unexpected, thirty minutes later. After a brief visit with Donna, Bob climbed into her high-backed wheelchair and motioned for Mike to give him a push. With that they disappeared down the long hallway. When they didn't return, I became furious. It wasn't only because they were treating hospital equipment like a toy and probably disturbing other patients, but I wanted to take Donna outside for some fresh air. And her chair wasn't available!

The nurses had seen me upset before, but they had never witnessed my full-blown Irish temper in action. I stomped out of Donna's room, looking up and down the hospital corridors. When I finally found them, I pulled Bob out of the chair and threw him on the floor. He didn't say a word; he only laughed. Laughter was his way of dealing with stupid behavior—and tragedy.

As always, Bob acted like nothing had happened. He picked himself off the floor, then asked me to take him to breakfast. He had a hunger for lobster tail and eggs, he said. Breakfast was the last thing on my mind at that point. I turned him down and he left with Mike in search of the perfect meal. Later that day, Bob left for Paris. Mike and I returned to Los Angeles.

It was on my next visit to Connecticut that Jean informed me that Donna was being transferred to a nearby convalescent hospital. Not being familiar with the facility, I had to check it out myself. As usual, I went unannounced.

From the moment I walked through the front door, I felt something was wrong. That feeling intensified on meeting the staff, and particularly the woman in charge. Their attitude shocked and appalled me. The supervisor, especially, was tough and coarse and difficult. I envisioned Donna in the hands of this insensitive person.

A tour of the place took me to the Head Trauma Unit. There I saw a young man coming out of a two-month coma. He was violent and hard to handle. He screamed obscenities at his mother, blaming her for everything. Seeing the poor woman, standing alone, helpless and confused, was a very sad sight. Rather than offering her assistance, a nurse turned to me and said, in a voice loud enough for the mother to hear, "See, they are never the same again." Her words, and the cold, hard look on her face told me everything I needed to know about the place. I returned immediately to Yale-New Haven to tell Jean what I had just observed. "Send Donna there and she'll never recover," I said. "She'll spend the rest of her life just the way she is now. You can't want that for her."

Jean listened, not really knowing what to say or do. She had to make what would undoubtedly be the most important and difficult decision in her life—and Donna's.

"Take her home with you," I pleaded, "where she'll be in her own bed, among familiar surroundings, and with people who love her. It won't be any more work for you. I'll provide 24-hour nursing care, whatever it takes." I was ready to promise the world, anything to keep Donna from going to the convalescent hospital. I couldn't bear the thought of her being under the control of that dreadful woman, and confined within such dreary, depressing conditions. The thought was frightening. I truly believed that transferring Donna to that facility would be the end of her. To my great relief, Jean agreed to my request. Then I faced another tearful departure. In my mind, having done as much as possible for Donna, I believed that I was about to say goodbye for a long time.

It was hard to pull away from her. In fact, I couldn't just tell her I was leaving and disappear. So I got her out of bed, held her upright within my arms, and we took a final walk around the hallways. At one point we reached a doorway with a sign that read "EXIT." Donna looked at it for a moment, then at me, and said, "Let's sneak out the back way now and you can take me to California with you." Her words were garbled, but I got the message.

How she remembered, I don't know, but she had recalled a time, years earlier, when I had walked out of St. John's Hospital in Santa Monica, following a bronchoscopy procedure. I left that hospital in the middle of the night with the help of Roy Noble, and now Donna wanted to do the same thing.

"You'll be getting out of here," I assured her. "You're going home with your mother. That's what is best for you now. You'll be in your own bed and. . . " She cut me off with her protests, thoughts spewing out in a frantic stream of words. Nothing I said was right. She simply didn't want to listen.

As I got her back to her room and into bed, she was sobbing wildly and clinging to me, as if for her life. She was afraid to let go, knowing I was leaving her behind. With the help of two nurses, I pulled away, for what I thought was the last time.

On the way to the airport, I told my cab driver, Arthur, that it would be a while before I returned to

Connecticut. "If I ever do return," I added, "it will be to take Donna back to California. There won't be any more good-byes because I can't go through that again." Then I slumped down in the back seat and cried unashamedly.

I was better once I got on the plane, feeling that I had done as much as possible to make things right for Donna. I wanted her to have a second chance, to see one more sunset, to feel the ocean breeze once again, to taste salt water and swim to her heart's content, to have the sparkle and enthusiasm for life she had when I first met her. I had a vision of Donna happily at home with her mother, in her own room, her own bed, with qualified, sensitive nurses to care for her. For the first time in months, I felt confident that Donna would be looked after in the way I felt she deserved. I couldn't wait to land and call everyone to spread the good news.

Two days later, I received a phone call from Jean to tell me there had been a change in plans. Donna was not going home. She was being transferred to the convalescent hospital.

I couldn't believe what Jean was telling me. Everything had been set, now this!

"Why, Jean?" I asked. "Why are you doing this to Donna?"

She had talked to the doctors at Yale-New Haven, she said, and they strongly recommended that Donna go to the nearby facility for rehabilitation.

"But I've been to that place," I told her. "I've seen what goes on there and, believe me, it's not in Donna's best interest." All I could picture was Donna under the control of the big, insensitive ward nurse and living alone in a small, isolated cubicle, cut off from everyone. I spelled out my fears to Jean, as calmly as possible, just as I had after my initial visit to the facility. "Donna's chances for recovery in that environment are not good," I reminded her. "She needs as much stimulation as possible. She needs to feel loved, and she's certainly not going to get that in an institution."

Jean and I talked at length on the phone, but I was unable to convince her to change her mind. She obviously felt the doctors knew better than I did, and perhaps on some level she was right. On this point, however, I knew Donna would never be given the full opportunity to recover with the convalescent hospital's impersonal "out to pasture" attitude. Her best and perhaps only chance would be with a more caring "hands on" approach.

In one final attempt to reverse Jean's decision, I had my mother telephone her. After talking with Clare for several minutes, it appeared that Jean was beginning to soften. By the time Clare motioned for me to join the conversation, I had an alternate suggestion to offer. Let us bring Donna to California to rehabilitate her in loving surroundings with us.

Jean's immediate reaction was a resounding "NO!" She was dead set against the idea. But Clare and I wouldn't give up. We went over and over the pros and cons of institutionalizing Donna verses outpatient care in a homelike atmosphere. Had I not seen the convalescent hospital firsthand, perhaps I wouldn't have been so adamant about my feelings. But my experience there, even though brief, had left such a negative impression that I could not risk placing Donna in the hands of people I did not respect.

Our pleading paid off. Jean finally agreed to let Donna come to California with one stipulation. If after one year Donna did not show noticeable progress, she would be returned to Connecticut.

Mother and I were elated. One year was a fair amount of time, we believed, to prove that Donna had a chance at recovery. At the end of one year, Donna's situation would be evaluated and, whatever the outcome, Jean would have the final say.

I immediately made arrangements to fly back to Connecticut. Then I contacted Yale-New Haven Hospital and Donna's doctor to set up a one-hour conference at 9:00 a.m. the following morning. "Have Donna's medical records available for me to pick up at that time. I am taking Donna to Los Angeles for treatment as authorized by her mother," I told them. When my plane landed in Connecticut that evening, I called the hospital to confirm our earlier conversation. It was important for the meeting to take place on schedule since I had return travel arrangements that had to be met.

On the morning of July 11, I walked into Donna's room precisely at 9:00 a.m. Donna's mother and sister, Carolyn, were already there, having arrived earlier to pack her belongings and prepare her for the trip. Donna appeared happy to be leaving, and we all chatted as we waited for the doctor to join us. Anxiously, I kept checking my watch. Arthur was waiting outside for us in his cab. A plane was standing by at Tweed-New Haven Airport to take us to New York's JFK for the cross-country flight. The minutes passed and still no doctor.

By ten o'clock I had run out of patience, and time. "I'm leaving," I said sharply, "and I'm taking Donna with me." Gathering Donna in my arms, we headed for the elevator. Jean and Carolyn followed behind with Donna's luggage.

As we reached the elevator the doors suddenly opened. There stood Donna's doctor. He stepped forward, and with a slight shrug of his shoulders he began to apologize for missing the meeting. I looked at him only briefly before we boarded the elevator. Then I turned and said, "Too little, too late!"

The elevator doors closed, leaving the doctor and Donna's medical records behind. We had a plane to catch.

CHAPTER 5

Dr. Ludwig Sees Hope

I was acting on impulse, letting my emotions run wild. Perhaps I should have shown more patience and not have taken Donna from the hospital as I did. At the time, however, I felt I had no choice. I simply couldn't wait a minute longer. The timetable had been set in place for our departure, and no telling what Jean might have done had we delayed. She had changed her mind once before about sending Donna away. I couldn't chance that happening again.

It was three months since the accident and Donna had greatly improved, however, she was still in no condition to travel. That point didn't fully sink in until we reached Tweed-New Haven Airport. The biggest problem was her inability to walk, or even stand on her own. She had no muscle strength whatsoever in her legs; they were like Jell-O. But I was determined that we walk together from the terminal to the plane, holding her firmly upright within my encircled arms just as we had walked the corridors of the hospital. The airline had offered a wheelchair but I refused it. Although it was impossible to know what Donna was thinking at times, I never once wanted her to feel that she was sick or impaired in any way. To me, it was important that Donna believed she was as normal as possible, and that she could do whatever anyone else could do.

Flying from Connecticut to JFK airport in New York, I began to suspect that I was alone on the journey. Donna kept looking out the window, but she did not comment about the landscape or buildings as they came into view. From time to time I tried to call her attention to various landmarks and points of interest, only to be met with silence. That wasn't like Donna at all. In the past, whenever we had traveled together, she had been quite verbal about everything she saw.

Communicating and sharing her thoughts had always been among Donna's strong traits. Now she sat staring into space. It was a blank stare, expressionless and indifferent, as if she had slipped back into a coma. Only now her eyes were open, seeing nothing. I watched her intently during the short flight. She showed no interest in anything.

Our arrival at JFK brought a repetition of what had taken place earlier at Tweed-New Haven, from the kind offer of a wheelchair to the long, strenuous walk, half carrying, half dragging Donna through the American Airlines terminal to our gate where we boarded our flight for Los Angeles. Along the way I introduced Donna to the friends I had made among the airline personnel during my many commutes to and from Connecticut. They were happy to finally meet the person who had generated so much activity over the past three months. It was wonderful to feel their kindness and warmth. One by one, they came up to Donna to wish her well.

Once we boarded the plane, we were ushered into the first-class cabin to our seats. I wanted to make sure we had lots of room and attention if necessary. We were offered something to drink—a choice of either orange juice or champagne. As I automatically ordered orange juice for both of us, Donna suddenly piped up and said, "Champagne!" I was momentarily stunned. Her head injury had wiped away much of her memory, but she apparently hadn't forgotten how to party.

The first few hours of the flight were uneventful. Donna sat quietly sipping her champagne and giving the impression she was watching a movie. I had no idea what was going on in her head, but she appeared to be enjoying the colorful moving pictures that flashed on the screen.

All of that changed when she announced she had to go to the bathroom. How quickly she had to get there, she didn't let on, but I didn't want to take any chances, emergency or not. We were about to experience her first bathroom encounter outside the hospital and I didn't want any slip-ups.

My first reaction was to ask one of the flight attendants to assist Donna, but I felt I'd had more experience in working with her and I was stronger. Guiding her down the narrow aisle, half carrying her, was one thing. Maneuvering her within the cramped cubicle, undressing and helping to balance her was another.

It seemed to take forever, partly because Donna and I were so clumsy and also because the space was so limited. Trying to calm and reassure her I talked non-stop. She responded with a burst of strange sounds, which must have raised more than a few eyebrows among the passengers on the other side of the locked lavatory door. The expressions on their faces when we finally returned to our seats left little doubt what they were thinking. Earlier, before we had disappeared, they were smiling and friendly. Now they wouldn't look at us. I couldn't let it go at that. Soon after I got Donna back into her seat and she fell fast asleep, I went to each of the passengers to explain why it had been necessary for me to be with Donna. Most responded with a compassionate smile or nod.

A familiar face was waiting when we arrived in Los Angeles. My mother had come to welcome us and offer her help. Donna recognized Clare immediately. She was so excited to see Clare that she broke away from me, staggered out of control and ran into a revolving glass door. She bounced back from the impact, then crumpled to the floor. She wasn't crying as I picked her up, and she didn't seem to be in pain, although she should have been. She simply looked at me oddly, as if to say, "What happened?" She didn't remember hitting the door. She didn't remember anything.

Clare had worked her way through the crowd of onlookers to reach Donna. Then she held her close. With Donna safe in my mother's arms, I left to retrieve our luggage.

Donna's new apartment in Manhattan Beach was only a few miles from the airport. Driving along the road bordering the ocean on that bright, summery July 11 day, I noticed there was a lot of activity on the beach. People sunning and playing in the sand, jogging along the water's edge and swimming in the surf. It had been three months since Donna had seen the beach. She loved being near the water, yet she said nothing about the ocean or the beautiful weather. She was as silent as she had been on the plane to New York, staring without comment.

She had the same non-reaction when we arrived at her apartment. Once inside, I helped her over to the living room windows that framed a panoramic view of the ocean. She stood looking out, not saying a word. Finally, I said, "Look, Donna, the ocean."

"How beautiful," she replied. "When did we get to Hawaii?" Clare and I looked at one another. "No, Donna," I said, "you're home. In Manhattan Beach."

She didn't believe me. She didn't remember having moved to Manhattan Beach. She didn't remember anything about Manhattan Beach. But she did remember visiting Hawaii before the accident and she was convinced she was there.

To help keep Manhattan Beach fresh in Donna's memory, I prevailed upon her neighbors, Christie and

Ron Cluff, to put up a large sign on the back of their card shop. It read: "Donna . . . Welcome to MANHATTAN BEACH, CALIFORNIA," with the last three words spelled out in big, bold letters. The sign was the first thing Donna saw each morning when she raised her shades, and it became a constant reminder to her of where she was. Eventually, she came to realize that it wasn't Hawaii.

The apartment really wasn't ready for Donna's arrival. Once Jean had agreed to let her daughter come to California, there had been no time to prepare, so I quickly recruited a team to help get Donna secure and settled in her new surroundings. Once again I called upon Betty and Roy Noble, and, of course, my mother, Clare. With their help, we activated utilities, stocked the refrigerator, rearranged furniture, and removed as many physical obstacles as possible so Donna would have a clear path through her house. We straightened up as best we could, then promptly got Donna into bed. Then we all looked at each other as if to say, "What now?"

To add to the confusion, prior to getting permission to bring Donna back to California, I had accepted an invitation to attend a dinner and wine tasting in Bordeaux, France, with Steve Wallace, a wine connoisseur, as the guest of the Mayor of Bordeaux. With Donna safely surrounded by Clare, Betty and Roy, Bob, Steve and I left the next day on our private jet.

However, once I arrived I was unable to get into the spirit of the occasion. As beautiful and festive as it was, my mind and heart would not permit me to leave Donna. My priorities were changing right on the spot. Less than twelve hours later, I boarded a commercial jet and returned to Los Angeles and Donna, realizing that a new Jim Connelly had a mission far more important and challenging than any he had ever undertook before—the work of Donna's recovery.

Once back in Manhattan Beach, even in the little time Donna had been with us, it became quite apparent that we would be confronted with enormous challenges. For example, while I was gone, Donna's brain had played a trick on her. When I arrived back in Los Angeles, I went immediately to Donna's apartment. Much to my chagrin, Donna didn't know me. When I said "I'm Jim Connelly," she would shake her head and say, "No, I'm looking for the *real* Jim Connelly." No matter what I said or did, Donna did not believe I was the "*real* Jim Connelly." Donna had developed a trust with my driver, Wayne Reeder, and used to tell him that when I entered the room, he was to stand behind me and signal to her if it was the "real Jim Connelly." Her inability to recognize me went on until August 23, when Donna accompanied me to my sister, Angela's birthday party. There were 100 people in attendance, all calling me "Jim." Later in the car on the way home, she looked at me and said in a loud, clear voice, "You must be the '*real* Jim Connelly' because even you couldn't pay 100 people to call you 'Jim Connelly.' That was amazing to me—all we had been through and somehow her brain had shut me out completely.

As my sister, Angela, soon pointed out, it was as if Donna's life was taking place within a three-foot circle. Beyond that, she was not connecting at all. Somehow, in some way, we had to expand her world beyond the "hula hoop." Thankfully, I was back in the loop.

Clearly, I wasn't thinking beyond that moment but, at the time, Donna's limitations weren't intimidating to me. I only knew that I had made a commitment to her rehabilitation and in the process, she would never be left alone or abandoned. She would receive the finest possible round-the-clock care. The goal of one year never crossed my mind. I could think only of the next minute, the next hour.

Perhaps that's why I was without an answer when Betty Noble asked about my plans for Donna. I had been so consumed with getting her safely back to California that I hadn't thought about much else.

"Daniel Freeman Hospital has an excellent program for head injury rehabilitation," said Betty. "And Dr. Barry Ludwig is a highly regarded neurologist, one of the best. You might want to see him for some direction."

Working as a nurse at Daniel Freeman, Betty knew almost everyone there. I respected her opinion and was grateful for her suggestion. She arranged an appointment with Dr. Ludwig's office for the following day.

It seemed things were beginning to fall into place. Donna's first day in California had been full. It had also been long and exhausting, both physically and emotionally. Now we looked forward to her first night in California, believing that once she was asleep, we too would get some rest. But sleep was not to be for any of us. Throughout most of Donna's care in the two hospitals, it had been necessary for her to use a catheter. The removal of the tubing had left her feeling as though she had to go to the bathroom all the time. The signals she received were usually false, but they hit her every few minutes all night long.

As time went on, we tried to be alert to Donna's needs, but that wasn't always possible. As she was getting stronger, quietly without saying a word, she would get herself out of bed and stagger through the unfamiliar territory of her small one bedroom apartment. She had no idea where the bathroom was located and so she would pass it by in her search. She didn't think to turn on a light. She made it to the front door, believing it was the bathroom door. Had she not bumped into things and made noise jiggling the lock, we wouldn't have known she was up and wandering about.

Through it all, Donna was sweet and good-natured, very much like a 100-pound newborn baby. We even managed a few laughs. She thought it was particularly funny when I told her she wouldn't find the bathroom beyond the front door, that it was in fact in the opposite direction. Finding the bathroom was one thing, but for her to do anything in the bathroom by herself was another.

Since the accident, someone had to be in charge of Donna's personal hygiene, and that person was me. We were going to meet with Dr. Ludwig later in the day, and I thought it would be a good idea for Donna to take a shower and wash her hair. I managed to get Donna into the bathtub, balanced between the sliding glass doors and the wall. My plan was to stand outside of the shower, using one arm to hold her up while she washed. My unrealistic goal was for me to remain dry. But as she began to lose her balance, I leaned in more and more to get a better hold on her. Now I had one leg in the tub and the shower was spraying me up to my shoulder. I realized she wasn't able to wash herself very effectively, so with my tennis outfit on, shoes and all, I joined her in the shower. I washed her, shampooed her hair and shaved under her arms.

When we were finished, I helped her out of the shower and as she was drying off, I was standing there, dripping wet in my clothes. She never even made a comment about what just happened.

After that challenging shower experience, baths became the order of the day and Donna luxuriated in them. They became her refuge, her safe haven. Even today she looks forward to that special time in her own private spa, using all sorts of sweet smelling bath salts and oils.

As frightening as it was to have Donna up on her own, I looked at it as a sign of progress. She was beginning to have some movement and mobility, which enabled her to get out of bed and move about. Even more encouraging, she didn't ask for assistance. The "old Donna" determination was surfacing.

Each day, long before sunrise, Donna was up to stay. Since the injury, her internal alarm clock seemed to be off by about four hours, going to bed about 5 or 6 p.m. and awakening around 4 a.m. For now that was fine because it gave her a chance to practice feeding herself and get ready for the drive to Dr. Ludwig's office at Daniel Freeman Hospital. While Donna was preparing for the day, I began to have a sick feeling in the pit of my stomach. Was I doing the right thing. Did I really want Donna involved again with the medical community? Would this be a repeat of the Connecticut experience?

It was too late to turn back now. Donna needed more than I could give her. And while I had lost all faith in the system's long-term care, Donna and I were in need of professional guidance. I also knew that I could not place Donna in a situation that was less than the very best for her full recovery. No matter who else was involved, I had to be in on the decision-making process. There would be no changing my mind about that.

The same merry-go-round of thoughts spun in my head as we waited to meet Dr. Ludwig. But once the door swung open and he introduced himself, my concerns and suspicions began to fade. Dr. Ludwig had a demeanor that inspired confidence. After months of adjusting to a new world with Donna, I was finally standing before a man who spoke with an open mind and a positive attitude. We had an instant rapport. Dr. Ludwig and I talked at length. He wanted to know all about Donna: her background, personality, how we came to meet, the events leading to the accident, and what had taken place over the past three months in the hospitals in Montana and Connecticut. At that point, he asked to see her medical records.

I was embarrassed to admit that I didn't have them, but he accepted my explanation with a smile. "Don't worry," he said. "We have Donna here with us now so let's move forward."

Moving forward meant running a series of essential tests on Donna. It was a fairly long procedure followed by his honest evaluation. According to Dr. Ludwig, Donna was "ataxic," which meant she could not control her movements on either side, although her right side was more affected. Additionally, at this time, she could not learn new information and retain it. Her slurred speech was also a factor. "With her unsteadiness, her memory impairment and confusion—that is, her marked cognitive problems—and her speech impairment, there is no way Donna can care for herself at this point." Dr. Ludwig suggested that she be admitted to Daniel Freeman's head injury unit right away.

While I greatly respected Dr. Ludwig's experience and opinion, I explained to him that I was against her being hospitalized. I preferred for her to be at home where her environment would be positive and upbeat, where she could learn to function in the real world. I then suggested we make Donna the first outpatient at Daniel Freeman to receive the inpatient program.

My suggestion did not sit well with the doctor. He looked directly at me for a long time, a perplexed expression on his face, as he mulled over my strange and unexpected request. Then he broke his gaze to look away, only to look back at me again and say, "Your idea might be a viable alternative." His voice was filled with uncertainty. Clearly he was not in favor of my plan. "You've lost confidence in the hospital system," he said. "I'm aware of that. For that reason I am going to agree, reluctantly, to give this experiment a try."

I breathed a sigh of relief. For the first time I felt that we had the support of a top professional, someone who would work closely with us toward our goal of full recovery and independence for Donna.

"Donna has so much to overcome," said Dr. Ludwig. "But the main thing, the obvious thing, is not to give up. Anyone who has a brain injury, if given the right therapy and motivation, along with good family and friend support, can make unbelievable progress— and perhaps even become independent again. I believe

Donna has a lot going for her. She is extremely motivated. That and your strong support are key elements to her recovery. Most families and friends disappear, especially spouses. Men seem to fade into the woodwork, while only mothers tend to stay involved. But I sense your dedication, and she will need that."

As part of Donna's new program, I promised that she would arrive promptly at the hospital five days a week for her daily eight hours of therapy, and provide transportation for her return home. I promised also to hire a registered nurse to be Donna's constant companion.

It had only been three months and four days since Donna's accident. Arriving at Dr. Ludwig's office I felt an unshakable apprehension. Now, leaving the hospital, I couldn't help but believe that things were finally falling into place for her recovery.

CHAPTER 6

"Don't Tell Me You're Irish, Too!"

From the shoulders down, Donna was beginning to gain some mobility and control. Although her right foot splayed noticeably outward, making her every movement awkward and unsteady, she could maneuver from room to room, even into the bathroom with some physical support. From the shoulders up, however, it was another matter. She had so much to overcome and progress was slow.

Because of Donna's difficulty in speaking and being understood, her first therapy session was scheduled with Rosemary Martinoff, a speech therapist at Daniel Freeman. Arriving at the hospital, Donna and I were directed to Rosemary's office. The door was open but I knocked anyway. Rosemary appeared instantly with a friendly smile and a warm welcome. It was a moment I will always remember. I felt we were on a roll having two positive people in the same organization. First Dr. Ludwig and, now, Rosemary. To think that Donna would be spending the coming months with people who saw the glass half full, rather than half empty, was not only comforting but exciting. I still light up when I think of Rosemary and that day in July of 1985 when we first walked into her office.

With Rosemary I never had the feeling we were one of many patients or that our time with her was limited. The atmosphere she created was casual and relaxed. She genuinely wanted to know about Donna and work with her to correct her pronounced speech deficiencies.

We wanted Rosemary to know that Donna had been a very successful salesperson and that speaking had been an important part of her life. Donna loved to talk and she wanted to contribute to the conversation. It was typical of Donna to speak rapidly whenever she became enthused. Meeting Rosemary, and the promise of working with her, thrilled Donna. In her excitement and eagerness to join in the conversation, a blur of slurred words came racing out of Donna's mouth.

Rosemary listened patiently, hearing more than we were actually saying in words. When it was her turn to talk, she explained that language and speech were not Donna's real problem. Donna had words, said Rosemary. Donna had sentences, and conversing was not a major area of deficiency for her. Donna's problem, Rosemary explained, was primarily one of poor articulation caused by her being hyper-nasal. "That sound comes from a lack of muscle coordination," said Rosemary. "A brain injury affects the nerves. In turn, they affect the muscles, resulting in poor circulation. We have a soft palate in the back of our throats. For the average person, it will close off very tightly and not allow air to go through the nose with most of our sounds. But when we say 'M' and 'N' and 'NG' it will rapidly open just for those sounds, the nasal sounds. It's a matter of the palate opening and closing, opening and closing, very rapidly."

I asked about Donna's slurring.

"That's a matter of articulation and speed," said Rosemary. "Speech is such a rapid function. Because Donna speaks rapidly anyway, especially when she is excited, enthusiastic, and probably agitated, it is difficult for her to monitor herself. Also, there is a snowball effect as she goes faster, faster, faster. She'll make one error, then another, then they all kind of magnify because her brain isn't telling her there's something wrong, so it doesn't self-correct."

Rosemary had Donna speak into a tape recorder, then listen to a playback of herself. Donna could not believe the voice she heard was her own.

"That's not unusual," said Rosemary. "When most people hear their voices played back they don't want to claim them. That's not *my* voice, they say." Rosemary smiled.

Rosemary recommended a prosthesis for Donna's soft palate to help correct her nasality and poor articulation. We made arrangements to see a prosthodontist and set up Donna's next appointment with Rosemary. I couldn't help but feel better knowing that Donna's condition, a neuro-muscular speech impairment called dysarthria, was under the care of an innovative, energetic, enthusiastic and wonderfully dedicated speech therapist. I was beginning to feel better, too, about having brought Donna to California.

The prosthodontist fitted Donna with a prosthesis to hold up her soft palate. The device hooked onto her top teeth and was almost like a surfboard down her throat. When Donna spoke slowly, she sounded terrific. But too often, she would slip into fast-talking and the device couldn't keep up with her. Donna simply spoke too fast. She found the prosthesis annoying, tweaking the back of her throat, which made her gag. Although Donna wore the prosthesis with determination for some time, almost six months, she ultimately put it away.

There were trips, too, to the optometrist. Donna was beginning to show concern about her appearance, and we took that as a healthy sign. She wanted to look good, and we wanted to help boost her self-esteem in any way possible. Thinking in a positive way was a major part of our plan for her long-term recovery, and she just didn't feel pretty wearing her old glasses. She had worn contacts since she was eleven years old, and she wanted to wear them now. But her eyes had changed since the accident, and we needed to update her prescription. Steve Wallace, a dear and valued friend, maintained an ongoing interest in Donna's recovery and recommended Dr. Cooperman. After an extensive eye examination with very sophisticated equipment, Dr. Cooperman was the first to say, "Donna, you are probably tired of hearing this, but you're going to get better." Hearing these words inspired great hope.

Donna liked her new contacts and her new look. But putting the lenses in and taking them out was impossible for her to do by herself. Her early attempts at trying were frustrating to her and anyone else who might be watching. It took her 45 minutes to put one in. Her coordination simply wasn't there. To help Donna, I brought in one of my employees, Ron Keibort, as a new member to our team. Ron arrived every morning just to put in Donna's contacts. He wore contacts himself and knew how to insert them. He was so patient with her, and so reliable, that I later asked him to be Donna's driver whenever I wasn't available.

Between appointments with the various doctors and specialists, Donna and I stayed close to Manhattan Beach. I was redoing her apartment to make it more comfortable and safe for her, such things as: putting in new windows that opened for fresh air; installing new carpet with double thick padding, to cushion her if she fell; adding motion detector lights outside; and putting flower boxes on her porch for her to enjoy. Because she couldn't sustain sleep for any length of time, she tired easily and napped often. We moved her bed into the living room where she could open her eyes and see the ocean. Her bedroom then became a guestroom for me, Clare, my sister, Angela, Betty or anyone who stayed overnight with Donna.

In the kitchen, the stove was stripped of its knobs to prevent Donna from accidentally turning on the burners. To be doubly safe, smoke detectors were installed in every room. We weren't taking any chances.

It was in the kitchen one day, while we were cooking a microwave breakfast, that something happened to amuse her. Donna then startled herself—and me. For months after the accident, no sound would come out when she laughed. But that day she laughed aloud. Donna was overcome with joy as she turned to me, a look of giddy amazement on her face. We hugged each other and jumped up and down in celebration.

Our days were busy and long. The nights were even longer. Donna continued to be up and down, wandering about—first to the bathroom, then from room to room. Time meant nothing to her so it was not unusual for her to wake me up and request something to eat or drink. More often than not, she just wanted to talk. After which, she would go back to bed, only to be up again moments later.

Sleeping did not come easily for Donna or for me. After the first night encounter when she tried to go outside in search of the bathroom, it was difficult for me to even nod off. No telling where she was or what she was up to. Additional locks had been installed on the door, but the fear that she would somehow get out or harm herself was always present. A few words of reason or caution should have kept her in bed. But for Donna, words had no lasting effect. Whatever was said to her was soon forgotten. Even mention of nighttime wanderings meant nothing to her in the morning. She simply couldn't remember.

After a few weeks of sleepless nights, my family and friends were beginning to show concern for me. I looked awful and I didn't care. I was now a member of the "silent society" of caregivers, those people who quietly give and sacrifice for their loved ones who need constant care. I had completely forgotten about me. I took a leave of absence from my job to do whatever was necessary to help Donna get better, and if that included 24 hours of my day every day, then so be it. I still felt that my being there with Donna made a difference for her. At this point I didn't know and probably wouldn't have accepted it anyway that Donna's life was a series of momentary events, each forgotten seconds after they occurred.

The fact that I had neglected my appearance didn't matter to me. But Donna's appearance did matter. She needed assistance washing, dressing, picking shoes and socks, otherwise she might put on dirty clothes or wear them inside out and select one pink and one purple sock to wear that day. I thought it was important for her to look good so she would feel good about herself, and I didn't want people laughing or staring at her. She had no fashion sense or awareness of what was appropriate to wear. She was not weather sensitive and if it were 90 degrees out, she might put on sweatpants, a long-sleeved sweater and a jacket; or conversely, if it were 50 degrees, I might find her in a bikini top and shorts. For me, it didn't matter. I wore the same old clothes for days, shaved whenever I had the energy, which wasn't often, and seldom ran a comb through my hair. Thank heaven for telephones. I could conduct much of my business without having to leave Donna's side.

I was as obsessive about her care at Daniel Freeman as I had been at Yale-New Haven Hospital. My back and forth flights to be with her were in the past, but that was about all that had changed. Although I had complete faith in the people who were working with Donna at Daniel Freeman, it was essential that I monitor every step of her progress. I insisted on receiving full daily reports about her and her curriculum from the hospital. I tried to back off a little, but that wasn't easy. I kept remembering Dr. Roth saying, "Without you, Jim, she can't make it." I didn't want to be known as one of those people who backed away from head injury patients, one of those persons who faded into the woodwork. I had heard over and over again from doctors, social workers and other people already caring for someone with head injury that it is a thankless job, frustrating, time consuming, lonely, expensive, and difficult to measure. But I wanted to be there for her always, no matter the cost. For nearly two weeks I had been at Donna's side around the clock. But as time went on I began to feel my own strength slipping away and their words ringing true.

It reached such a point that by July 25 I was emotionally, mentally and physically exhausted. I had to get away if only for an hour or two. I needed to be in a totally different environment. I wanted to share some time with new and interesting people and engage in stimulating conversation. I wanted and needed to stop being a full-time caregiver for just a few hours.

The impulse hit me to arrange an impromptu party aboard the company yacht, a beautiful 60-foot dual engine Chris Craft. I contacted my friend Bruce Bennetts and asked him to make some phone calls. "I don't care who's there," I told him, sounding rather desperate, "just get some people together." He said he would take care of it.

My mother agreed to stay with Donna while I was away. Where the day had gone, I had no idea. I had been up all night with Donna—she was in and out of bed about every two minutes—and I'd had my hands full from then on. When Clare arrived it was 3:45 and the party was set to begin at 4:00. She took one look at me and frowned.

I hadn't showered, shaved, combed my hair or changed clothes since the day before. Red wine stains ran down the front of my blue shirt. I was somehow oblivious to my appearance in my rush to leave. I was a stickler about being on time and all my friends knew it.

As I jumped into my car and headed north along the stretch of coastal road leading from Manhattan Beach to the Marina, I kept checking my watch. It was almost 4 o'clock. The next thing I knew a police car was behind me, signaling for me to pull over. Rather than waiting for the officer to approach me, I bounded from my car and rushed to him. "You're right, I'm wrong," I hurriedly confessed. "I don't have my license or registration so you're going to have to trust me." It's a wonder I wasn't shot, or held off at gunpoint. Storming a policeman is not a smart thing to do. But I wasn't thinking, and I certainly wasn't being arrogant. I wanted only to speed things up.

My forthright attitude must have caught the officer off guard. At least that's the reaction I got as he stood speechless staring at me. Finally, he shook his head and said, "This is most unusual." With that he took my name and address, wrote out a ticket for speeding, and let me go. Had he phoned to verify the information I had given him, I would have been held up even longer, but he didn't. For some unknown reason, he trusted me—despite my appearance with the wine stains on my shirt.

By the time I parked and made it to the dock where the yacht was moored, it was 4:10 p.m. The motor was running and a dozen or so people stood on deck, waiting for me. I raced up the gangplank and shouted, "Let's go!"

As I climbed the stairs to the deck, I made eye contact with someone I had never seen before. She was sitting across the table with another woman near the back of the boat. I walked over to her, my eyes still fixed on hers, and said almost challengingly, "Don't tell me you're Irish." She stared at me as if to say, "Who is this person?" And who could blame her? I looked like a wild man and acted half-crazy. But she didn't even blink. She simply answered, "My name is Kate Kelly." Upon hearing that, I banged my fist on the table and blurted, "The last thing I can afford to do is fall in love!" I wanted to stay, but I had already embarrassed myself. Without saying another word, I turned quickly and stormed to the front of the yacht to join the others.

It was good being with familiar faces, old friends again. We laughed, filled our glasses with Dom Perignon, and waived at passing boats as we slowly made our way toward the main channel. It was a gorgeous afternoon, and everything seemed right with the world again, at least for the moment. But no matter how I tried, I could not get Kate Kelly out of my mind.

What was happening to me? I had known a lot of women in my life, but never had the feeling that swept over me on seeing Kate. "Love at first sight" happened only in the movies, as far as I was concerned. But this was real. Something inside me was generating a feeling of completeness. Kate was more than just beautiful; there was something about her—serenity, dignity and balance. I didn't even know her and yet I wanted her to be a part of my life. I had to see her again!

She was still sitting with the other woman as I made my way to the back of the yacht. The closer I got to them the broader my smile became. I was feeling so good, and it wasn't the champagne. "I want to thank you both for coming today," I said, leaning over between them, gently touching their shoulders. Then I walked away again, hoping I hadn't embarrassed myself even more than the last time. For some reason, I turned momentarily to look back at Kate. Our eyes met again. She was watching me and she had a puzzled expression on her face. I heard her say, "We should be thanking you for inviting us."

I didn't hear them approaching. They had followed me to the bow of the boat where I stood away from the other guests. A fresh sea breeze cooled my face while the music from the overhead speakers blended into the soft slapping of water against the hull. In the near distance the rocky breakwater signaled we were quickly approaching the open expanse of Santa Monica Bay.

Who was this Kate Kelly, and how did she come into my life? The whole story didn't come out right away, or even that day, but over time I learned that she and the other woman, Maureen Kelly, were sisters. Maureen worked at the Marina City Club along with my friend, Bruce Bennetts, and she had seen me around the Club. Little did I know then that Maureen had felt for some time that Kate and I should meet, believing that we had, in her words, "a similar sense of humor." There was one problem, however. Kate lived in Indiana. Although she had come to California to visit her sister, the odds of our meeting were extremely slim, especially after all that had happened over the past few months. The fact that I called Bruce to arrange the get-together on the yacht was serendipitous.

I didn't want to talk about Donna and all that was going on in Manhattan Beach. I had come to the Marina to relax for a few hours, if possible, not to relive the recent past. But Kate was so special I felt I had to be up-front with her. She had to know what had prompted me to say, "The last thing I can afford to do is fall in love."

Kate listened patiently as I told her about Donna's accident and my commitment to help her get better. Outside of my immediate family, she struck me as being a person who clearly understood the stress and strain stemming from the April accident. It wasn't what she said. It was her actions, her eyes and body language,

ONE MORE SUNSET

that told me she could relate to the pressures. I really didn't have to explain much. That drew me even closer to her. She knew. She truly knew. That came out when she told me about a very dear friend, a stunt pilot by avocation. She was at the air show ten years before and had witnessed the accident that caused his partial paralysis. They had been very close, and although she didn't say it, I felt the role of caregiver was one she knew well. There was more. Her father had died at age 57 only six months earlier. And her youngest brother, Sean, had Down syndrome. It was obvious we had more in common than being Irish, and a similar sense of humor.

The cruise seemed all too short. Before either of us knew it, we had talked the time away and we were back at the Marina. Then came another dramatic change in my life when I asked Kate if she would join me for dinner the following evening. Suddenly I was thinking about spending more time away from Donna.

"I can't do that," Kate answered, rather apologetically. "I'm going to the races at Del Mar."

"How about the next night?" I asked quickly. Where I was going with this I didn't know. The fact is, I didn't know that much about her. Was she married? Did she have children? Did she have a current boyfriend? If she had said yes to any of those questions it wouldn't have mattered. I would have told her to bring her husband, children or significant other or whomever along with us. Her possible involvement with someone else didn't mean a thing to me. She simply made me feel special, and for a brief few hours she had taken me away from all that was going on in my life.

Her response to my question brought another negative. "I'm going home," she said. "Back to Indiana."

"Well, change your plans," I countered.

She didn't answer, and I could see by the look on her face that she wasn't accustomed to anyone telling her what to do. My hard-nosed persistence wasn't paying off, so I restated my plea in a gentler, more caring way. "If you have one of those funny airline tickets, I'll gladly make up the difference," I said. I was practically begging.

Kate smiled, and agreed to stay one extra night. That was all I needed. I went back to Donna's apartment with renewed spirit.

Now I was thinking about what to do on our date. The short time we had spent on the yacht seemed frozen in time. Could I recapture those same feelings? I wondered. What could I do for an encore to make our next encounter even more memorable? She seemed to enjoy my company and being aboard the yacht. Why not do it again, only this time without all the others?

Two afternoons later we boarded the yacht to the same music, the same chef-prepared buffet, the same champagne, and the same calm waters of the Marina. Only now my hair was combed, my face was freshly shaved, my clothes were spotless and, except for the crew, we were alone together.

As we eased out of the Marina and into the open water, we settled back to enjoy the view of the bay. It was another sparkling afternoon. With Kate at my side, I was feeling almost reborn. How wonderful she made me feel! I turned to look at her and she calmly asked, "How often do you do this?"

Her remark brought me back down to earth, but it was a fair question. It took a crew to get the yacht moving. The truth was I may have entertained on the yacht, but I'd never moved it out for one person. Until now, I had never wanted to take it out for only me and someone else. I looked at her quite proudly and replied, "Never."

My honest confession set the tone for the rest of the cruise. We lazily cruised the Marina as we sipped champagne and ate fresh sea bass prepared right on the boat. After the meal we sat on the bow of the yacht,

94   ONE MORE SUNSET

watching the sunset, content just to sit next to each other, breathing in the ocean smells. But as we got closer to the dock, I wanted to be closer to her. I had gently hugged her during the cruise, but now I wanted more. In spite of the reality of Donna's tragedy, my feelings for Kate took me away.

It was dark now. Slowly we walked up to the dock and the first mate secured the boat. I was about to suggest we get more comfortable when she said, "I have a good idea. Why don't we take a nice walk?" That wasn't what I had in mind, but I agreed anyway.

We strolled leisurely along the glittering waterfront past the Ritz Carlton Hotel, then back to the Marina City Club complex of curving high-rises, where the yacht was moored. In the near distance stood a low, sprawling building with picture windows overlooking the Marina. "That's my restaurant, Mulligan's," I said. "Why don't we go in and have a nightcap?"

Kate smiled. "Fine," she answered.

Her simple one word reply switched on a little light in my head. Once again I was filled with hope and anticipation. But when she ordered club soda instead of a drink, I knew the evening was over.

The next day Kate returned to Indiana. Before she left, however, I told her I wanted to see her again. I *had* to see her again. Kate had become so important to me, not only to my sanity but to my survival as well. It all seemed so incredulous that I could have developed such strong feelings for someone in such a short time, but I did.

It was impossible for Kate to know that at the time. How could she? Despite our long talks, I couldn't completely open up to and chance scaring her even farther away. And so, understandably, she was non-committal about coming back to visit me. She said, "Let me know you're thinking about me and I'll think about it."

Thinking about her? Despite all else that was going on in my life, she was constantly on my mind. To let her know just how much, each day I sent her something—flowers, candy, champagne or a special telegram message.

The owner of the local flower shop loved me. So did the proprietor of every gift shop in Manhattan Beach, as well as the telephone company. Between the daily deliveries, there were phone calls. If Kate weren't home, I'd leave messages and play love songs. Calling became habitual, even from the car. I'd hear a romantic song on the radio and quickly dial Kate so I could play it for her.

As with everything else that meant the world to me, I became passionate about Kate. I couldn't lose her. She had to come back to me—if only for a visit.

CHAPTER 7

100 Days
Since the Accident

It was now one hundred days since the accident. In early August, nearly a month after Donna's first visit to Daniel Freeman Hospital, it was clear to me I needed help. I finally admitted I couldn't do it alone, so I hired a companion for her. Dr. Ludwig had recommended sometime back that I do so. Perhaps I had waited too long. My strong commitment to Donna was being challenged not only by mounting business pressures but also by an ongoing long-distance pursuit of Kate. I felt like I was being pulled in all directions at once. What distressed me more than anything, although I failed to acknowledge it at the time, was my sudden attitude toward Donna. Too often I found myself losing my patience. It was basically "24/7" as the hospital staff referred to such a schedule: 24 hours a day, seven days a week. Looking back, I clearly see the signs of my exhaustion.

There were times when the pressure was almost unbearable and I needed to get away. As Donna became more awake and aware, she began to talk non-stop. Many times I begged her for silence. Who was the patient here? I began to wonder. It was too easy to forget that barely four months had passed since Donna had been the victim of a horrifying accident. When it crossed my mind, I tried not to think about it. What about my own needs? My own life?

Anyone who came in touch with me during those dark days probably thought I should have been committed. It wasn't that I didn't have relief from time to time. My mother, Clare, was a lifesaver, ready to step in on a moment's notice. And I could count on free time several nights a week. Wednesdays were set aside for my sister, Angela, and her husband Hugh. They would drive to Manhattan Beach, pick up Donna and take her to their home in Santa Monica for dinner. At other times they took her out to popular restaurants, knowing how Donna loved to experience new places and a variety of cuisine. Donna enjoyed Angela and Hugh, and I knew she was in very responsible hands with them.

Another person I fully trusted was my younger sister, Kathe. Every Thursday afternoon following work, Kathe drove from her office in Los Angeles to Manhattan Beach to take Donna to dinner. Because Donna had difficulty remembering from day to day, or even what day it was, Kathe made a game of their get-togethers. She would have Donna say to her, "If it's Thursday, you must be Kathe. If you are Kathe, it must be Thursday." From there, Donna was able to determine that "yesterday was Wednesday and tomorrow will be Friday."

The weekly dinners with my sisters were for Donna's sake as well as mine. I wanted her days and weeks to have some continuity. Repetition was very important, not only to keep her mind active but to help stir her memory. And I wanted her to have something to look forward to every week. It also gave me a much-needed break.

If Donna was moving forward, however, I couldn't see it. I was too close. Too many hours and days together blinded me to whatever progress she was making. I began to look at her only by the light of each new day,

ONE MORE SUNSET

because she remembered nothing from the previous 24 hours. There were no yesterdays on which to build because of the loss of her short-term memory. I didn't want to, but I began to doubt Donna's future. Somehow, I had to regain a positive attitude and outlook. I felt like I was back managing the Beverly Wilshire Hotel again, trained to see only what was wrong.

Thank God for Vinetta Taubert, a registered nurse. It was on the strong recommendation of Betty and Roy that I brought her to Manhattan Beach to be with Donna. Although Donna was an enormous challenge, I could sense Vinetta was capable of taking care of anything that came her way. A strong, young woman, she could certainly handle Donna physically. She was also very resourceful and energetic. She could work Donna's brain with conversation as well as creative activity.

Vinetta was a highly qualified professional, but it was important that she not look like "a nurse." I recall telling her early on, "Dress in casual clothes because Donna is not sick. I don't want her to think of herself as being ill, because she is not. She is recovering from a severe head injury." Vinetta agreed with the plan. "Since we didn't want the white nurses uniforms," recalled Vinetta of her early days with Donna, "I wore my everyday clothes, which I think made Donna feel more comfortable. But she was having a problem with her own clothes. She was relearning how to dress herself all over again, and it wasn't easy for her. Donna put things on backward or inside out, or else they would have big spots on them from the day before. The colors and patterns she picked usually clashed. Nothing seemed to match or go together. To help her remember where certain articles of clothing were located, we labeled all cabinets and dresser drawers."

Although the small four-room apartment felt like

home to Donna, she still had difficulty going from one room to the other without getting lost. She would still confuse the bedroom with the bathroom or walk through the kitchen thinking she could get to her closet. While she still struggled to visualize the apartment layout, physically she was getting stronger. While there was still a noticeable unsteadiness in her gait as she moved about, she was gaining strength in her legs and she no longer needed anyone to assist her. Still, because of her poor memory, she needed constant supervision.

Vinetta wouldn't let Donna out of her sight. She couldn't. As many times as Donna had been to the hospital for therapy sessions, she had no idea where to go once she got there. She couldn't get from the parking lot to the therapy wing, and as important as food was to Donna, she couldn't get to the lunchroom. Following the sessions, they took long walks into the community around the hospital, then along the streets of Manhattan Beach. We hoped that with repetition Donna would begin to recognize buildings, landmarks, and signs that would transfer into her long-term memory and permit her to eventually find her own way.

While Donna was at therapy during the day, I was able to spend time in my office. When Donna got home, walking was an activity we shared. We would make our way out to the end of the Manhattan Beach pier to watch the sunset. In the beginning when Donna struggled to walk on her own, we started out doing the elephant walk. I would hold her in front of me, my arms locked securely around her waist, and I would nudge her legs, one at a time, moving mine at the same time. Even though this was challenging, I knew that our continual effort would help Donna relearn to walk. In time, we were able to walk side by side with just one of my hands holding the collar of her jacket. Still unsteady, the second I let go she would veer to her left. In addition, she didn't feel or recognize curbs or slants in the pavement, which threw her off balance. But she was improving and the neighbors and local merchants noticed too. Whenever they spotted us they would signal with a thumbs up sign.

Reaching the end of the pier, Donna and I would stand at the rail to watch the sun sink below the horizon. The display of colors, while often brilliant, made no impression on Donna. She had always loved sunsets and now she simply stared. I was beginning to wonder if she'd really ever see another one.

It was difficult to know what was going on in Donna's mind. She was undergoing therapy, in one form or another, from morning 'til night. What she received at the hospital five days a week, Vinetta continued at home. As Vinetta remembered, "Donna had no real leisure time. She had so many different therapy groups to go to that it was all work, work, work for her. On the weekends we tried to do fun things, but even they became a type of therapy."

Part of Donna's fun was riding a stationary bike. She enjoyed biking before the accident so it seemed only natural to get her a bike she could ride at home. We set it up in her living room and she couldn't wait to get on it. She would ride it for 15 minutes, get off, then start all over again. She would forget she had just ridden it. This would go on for maybe a total of two hours because at this time she still did not feel exhaustion.

The repeated stints on the bike strengthened Donna's legs considerably as well as helped to improve her coordination and balance. Although she still had a problem with her right leg, she was walking straighter now and the unsteadiness in her gait was disappearing. She was also taking naps more frequently and her appetite had increased. We chalked it up to her new workout activities.

The daily naps did help to fill up her day. Her biggest enemy was boredom. "She had a firecracker in her," recalled Roy. "She wanted everything to be exciting or she would get bored. Even if she had enjoyed something, she'd forget she had done it." For Donna, eating was entertainment and sleep was an escape.

She was nibbling constantly and had gained not only the weight she had lost after the accident but added nearly 20 pounds more. She now weighed 127 pounds and what she saw in the mirror did not make her happy. Donna had always been fit and trim. Suddenly, she was taking on a fuller, softer look.

The mirror revealed another surprise: her skin was no longer clear and smooth. Was it the food she was eating, her new less-than-selective diet?

Whatever it was, Donna didn't like what was happening to her. She never had skin problems before. Nor had she ever been so continually cold. Even on the warmest days, she bundled herself in sweaters and jackets. "It's because of the damn accident," she would say. "It's because I was lying so long on the ice." She didn't remember lying on the ice, but she had heard the story many times.

Donna never complained, at least not right away. In fact, at Daniel Freeman Hospital she became upset when the patients in her group therapy sessions talked in a negative way. "They are always complaining because they can't remember their accidents or what happened to them," she said one day. "I tell them, 'Who wants to remember any of that or think about the pain? Just be happy!'" Her upbeat attitude earned her the nickname of "Pollyanna." But her smile quickly faded when she heard the therapists refer to their patients as being "disabled." Donna detested the word. "I am not disabled!" she said emphatically.

Each day Donna was faced with new obstacles, unforeseen hurdles that made her life that much more difficult. While she was at therapy it seemed the spotlight was on her shortcomings and she was becoming more and more aware of what she couldn't do. Had it not been for her remarkable inner strength, I doubt she would have been able to cope with such challenges, such as relearning how to make change when buying a cup of coffee or how to tie her shoes. As Betty Noble later confided, "Donna probably didn't even realize it, but that was a very difficult time for her. Perhaps it was a blessing that her short-term memory was virtually non-existent."

More than anything else at this time, I believed Donna needed order and positive support in her life. A bulletin board seemed like such a simple thing, but it was worth a try and turned out to be a lifesaver. A large framed chalkboard was hung near her front door where she could easily see it. Each morning we wrote the day and date, things to do and messages. Donna called it her "reminder board." Inspirational messages were also posted such as: *Inch by inch, life is a cinch; We are not in a hurry; We love and respect each other.* Seeing them always brought a warm smile to Donna's face and helped her face the day.

Whatever progress we were making to brighten Donna's life was interrupted with the arrival of one of her brothers. Jimmy had come from the East Coast to visit his sister in California for the first time. He came with good intentions, I'm sure, but his presence had a shattering effect on Donna. He moved too quickly for her, talked too fast, asked too many questions that she couldn't answer, and brought newfound friends from the beach to her apartment to party. Donna simply couldn't cope with the noise, the pressures or the confusion. After only a few days, I bought him a ticket and sent him home. Following her brother's departure, Donna said, "If you see anyone coming with suitcases, send them to a hotel!"

It wasn't much later that Donna woke up one morning with a terrifying pronouncement. "If I wouldn't get the lifeguard in trouble," she said sadly, "I'd walk into the ocean and commit suicide."

Donna's voice therapist, Rosemary, had warned us early on to watch for signs of depression in Donna. It was common with head injury patients, she had explained, and sooner or later Donna would probably be affected. "It may not happen for a while," said Rosemary, "because Donna has so many people lifting her spirits, but Donna's depression will come."

Several days later, my family, members of the A Team, and I met with a group of Donna's therapists to discuss and evaluate her progress to date. Actually, there wasn't much of a discussion since the meeting was rather cut and dry. We were basically in attendance to hear the prognosis for Donna's future.

In a word, we were told that Donna's condition was hopeless. "She will never be able to remember or function in a normal way," we were informed.

I was stunned. It had only been a little more than four months since the accident, and Donna had already made enormous strides. She hadn't been able to do anything when she came out of her coma. She was like a newborn baby, exploring the world for the first time. Now she was talking and walking, and without assistance. How could they call her *hopeless*? What did they really know and whose evaluation chart were they using?

My eyes filled with tears as we left the therapists and slowly made our way out to the hospital parking lot. We walked in silence, too choked with our own emotions to speak. There was nothing to say, really, but with each step I felt a new determination to prove the therapists wrong. I would double my efforts. I would do whatever necessary to make Donna well again, but I would definitely not give up on her. She was not hopeless! There would be another sunset. I have always believed it's not what happens to you, but what you do about it that matters.

CHAPTER 8

Donna's Diary

It was important for me to meet with Dr. Ludwig immediately about Donna's prognosis. There were too many questions and I needed answers. Why was Donna so cold all the time? Why was she gaining so much weight? Why was she having skin problems? What could we do to get her out of her depression?

Several of my questions related directly to Dilantin, a drug she was first given at Yale-New Haven Hospital to control convulsions and seizures, such as she had experienced shortly after coming out of the coma. She was still taking the drug as a precautionary measure.

When doctors administer or prescribe drugs to patients, we too often accept them without knowing the potential dangers or side effects. During emergencies, as in Donna's case, time becomes a factor. Administer first, ask questions later. But no one asked Donna's doctor in Connecticut about possible side effects, nor was the information volunteered once it had been administered and prescribed for long-term use. Perhaps doctors aren't totally at fault. Why cause the patient and family members needless concern when in the majority of cases the patient may not react adversely at all? However, when in doubt, ask.

Unfortunately, Dilantin carried a long list of possible side effects, including confusion, drowsiness,

105

anxiety, headaches, skin rash, red or flaking skin, slurred speech, a staggering walk, weight gain, and much more. Many of them related directly to conditions experienced by Donna.

My first reaction was to immediately take Donna off the drug, but my sister, Angela, said "no!" She had researched Dilantin and had learned that it is not a drug that can be stopped suddenly. Once it is in a person's system, she said, it has to be withdrawn slowly. And so after confirming Angela's findings with Dr. Ludwig, we began a program of gradually weaning Donna off Dilantin. She had been taking two tablets (called infatabs) a day. Now she would take one. Soon that would be cut to one-half, and, finally, to none.

As much as I wanted to blame all of Donna's problems on Dilantin, I could not. In talking about the other patients in her therapy sessions, Donna had mentioned that they all seemed to be either out of shape or on the heavy side. She was very conscious of their weight as well as her own. I thought nothing about it at the time. Nor did I connect her remark with her condition as she began to put on pounds. But the head injury connection was there. Only her drowsiness and skin problems, as I soon learned, were directly related to the Dilantin.

There is a mechanism in the brain that tells you when you feel hungry or full, triggering an impulse that says "EAT" or you've had enough, "STOP!" If that mechanism is injured, there is oftentimes a weak signal or none at all. You never feel full, so you keep eating. It isn't that you have forgotten you've eaten, it's as if you haven't eaten at all. So there is an urge to eat and eat and eat. I saw this phenomenon firsthand when Donna ate three full dinners on Thanksgiving and promptly threw up on me.

Learning that her eating was related to her head injury had Donna in an uproar. "I am so mad," she fumed. "That will ruin my life!" She began pacing the room, back and forth. When she finally stopped, she said with great conviction, "Oh, no it won't. I know what I'll do. I'll eat hardly anything from now on—only fruit and water!" Knowing Donna as I did, she meant it. More and more we were discovering that the accident had no effect on her determination.

Donna's bundling up to keep warm had nothing to do with Dilantin, as I believed, or her lying injured for hours on the ice, as she thought. It seems that people who have had major surgery or injury tend to be very sensitive, and often intolerant, to temperature changes, even the least little chill. For Donna to be so constantly cold in the summertime did not seem right. But hearing the doctor's explanation made sense. The breezes that blew in off the ocean were a welcome relief to everyone but Donna. In time, we were told her sensitivity to cooler air would fade. Another concern was Donna's too frequent trips to the bathroom. She didn't complain, she simply disappeared at all hours of the day and night to remain behind the closed bathroom door, often for extended periods.

Sometimes she might perform her Erno Laszlo skin care ritual three times in a row. Once after being in the bathroom nearly half an hour, she came out into the living room with her face covered in a gooey pink mask, forgetting there were guests waiting for her.

Many other trips to the bathroom were false alarms, not directly related to her head injury but rather to her hospitalization. While she was in a coma, it was necessary for Donna to be catheterized. After the tube was removed, Donna had little control of her bladder and she often had a false sensation to go to the bathroom. She had experienced months of incontinence, particularly whenever she laughed, sneezed, coughed or cried. It was necessary for Vinetta to carry extra pairs of underwear for such times. Even after she gained control, she continued to feel pressure, real or imagined, of having to urinate.

It was Dr. Ludwig who suggested that we cut back on Donna's therapy sessions, from five days a week to two. The feeling was that Donna, with her enthusiasm to get better, had been pushing herself too hard. The negative repetition of what Donna considered "stupid, childish activities" had already taken its toll on her. Even a person with a head injury experiences stress.

A cutback had actually been suggested weeks earlier. As Rosemary recalled, "Donna had been working so hard in her therapy sessions. It must have been terribly monotonous for her. Every day was basically the same—same place, same people, same exhausting exercises. So I said to her one day, 'Let's take a little vacation, Donna. You'll come back refreshed.' Well, she wouldn't hear of it. Her reply was a definite 'No, I've got to keep doing this.'"

My meeting with Dr. Ludwig had been productive, and as we ended our talk I felt somewhat encouraged. Before leaving, however, I asked if there was anything more I could or should be doing for Donna. "Just keep up the support," he replied. "Support is the key. At this point she needs time, patience and love."

Donna's "relaxed schedule" away from the hospital opened new avenues for her. At the suggestion of my sister, Kathe, we added another member to the team. Dr. Rex, a visualization expert in Los Angeles, was retained to work with Donna to help improve her short-term memory. Roy Noble drove her three days a week to his office in Los Angeles.

Donna got off to a fast start with mental exercises that had her visualizing the location of countries around the world, along with their capitals. Thanks to her father, who taught them to her as a game when she was a child, she was able to retrieve the information from her long-term memory.

On free days, Donna took to her stationary bike with a vengeance, riding it morning, noon and night.

Angela noticed that Donna had begun to walk with her head tilted to the side and with "tight" shoulders. Even though Donna didn't complain, Angela arranged an appointment with a chiropractor in Beverly Hills to ease her shoulder tightness and help keep her head and neck in line. But Donna went only once, not wanting to become tied to another doctor. "I was sorry she quit," said Angela, "but once she makes up her mind, that's it." Over time, Donna began to "let go" and her shoulders did too. I think lightening her therapy sessions had a lot to do with her becoming more relaxed.

Physical exercise became Donna's ally, paying dividends by strengthening her legs and increasing her endurance. She began walking straighter and for longer periods. Wherever she went, her camera went with her. "She shot a roll a day," said Vinetta, "taking pictures of everything . . . people, places, things, especially flowers. She loved flowers of all kinds. Oh, yes, and now sunsets."

Of course, getting the film developed was a big event. Donna was treated very well at the camera shop because we were there on a daily basis and she felt at home around the cameras, having worked for Kodak. If being around photo equipment stirred memories for Donna, so did the pictures she took. They became extremely helpful in expanding her short-term memory by showing where she had been a day or two before.

Another frequent stop on Donna's walks through Manhattan Beach with Vinetta was the beauty salon, where they would have their nails done. The people at the salon were much like those at the camera shop. They knew of Donna's accident and were very supportive and friendly. Donna was always welcomed with smiles. It didn't seem to matter, however, if she knew anyone, as she made her way around town, because she wasn't easily intimidated and she loved to meet new people. If she was self-conscious about her injury, she didn't show it. Perhaps it was her Pollyanna spirit. More likely, it was her tremendous courage.

Donna's interest in her appearance was a good sign since people who are depressed or ill for long periods generally lose interest in how they look. Fortunately, Donna's concern began almost from the moment she arrived back in California when she insisted on contact lenses rather than glasses. Now her nails were important to her. She believed they were the one thing she could control, and she wanted them to be long, extra long and beautiful. She even began carrying a jar of Barielle cream with her wherever she went. It wasn't unusual for her to apply the cream six or seven times a day, massaging her nails constantly.

She took the same interest in her complexion. I had introduced Donna to Erno Laszlo skin care products soon after we met in 1982, but it wasn't until she began taking Dilantin that she developed skin problems and my mother, Clare, took over. "She was breaking out terribly," said Clare. "I took one look and said, 'I must help her with her complexion.'"

My mother had the franchise for the Laszlo skin care line at her shop in the Marina City Club, and she worked closely with Donna to bring back her complexion. Donna's bathroom was filled with special soap, creams and lotions, astringents and powders that had to be lathered and applied in a precise order and manner several times daily. Almost immediately we saw improvement. As with almost everything else Donna did, the routine would be repeated many more times than necessary because she could not remember having already done it.

As Donna became more confident about her appearance, eating out and shopping became enjoyable diversions for her and Vinetta. They usually walked to local restaurants and stores, but to places outside of Manhattan Beach they were driven and assisted at various times by a number of special people: Jami Simon, Wayne Reeder, Ron Keibort and Alice Dandridge.

At one point in time, Donna's adventures with eating accelerated when she began reading the Los Angeles times restaurant reviews and advertising section. Exotic and third world country eateries particularly caught her attention. Prior to going, she would research the country and read all about their food and customs. Roy was her willing and faithful companion on these treks all over Southern California. Many times they'd go hunting for these off-the-beaten path places, get lost for hours and end up at some other unusual café. Occasionally, Donna would be disappointed with the food or the environment and she and Roy would immediately get a doggy bag and head home. I think Roy deserves a special place in heaven for his willingness and patience to always acquiesce to Donna's request. I often told him it was ok to say "No", but he never did.

Although Donna loved going to restaurants, eating was not her priority. She loved the ambiance, the people and the ritual. Somehow, her pledge to cut back on her food intake had remained locked in her memory. No matter how tempting various items on the menu might have been, her worry over weight gain was stronger. Said Vinetta, "Wherever we went she settled for fruit salad. After the accident Donna was not a big eater, but now she barely picked at her food so there were always leftovers to take home. She was so conscious of the other people in her therapy group who had no control over how much they ate, and she didn't want that to happen to her."

At home, Donna became a whiz at making salads, mixing all kinds of fruits together into colorful and tempting displays. Once she proudly finished the preparation, however, she seemed to lose interest in eating. She would take a bite or two, then put the salad in the refrigerator for future nibbling. It was odd to open her refrigerator and see dish upon dish, each with only one or two uncovered bites of moldy food on it. Because Donna couldn't smell, she couldn't tell when food went bad, not even milk. Weekly, our challenge was to clean the refrigerator and convince Donna to throw it away.

Vinetta would occasionally take Donna into the kitchen for what she called "therapeutic cooking." These sessions were less to cook actual dishes than to see how Donna followed instructions and to test her patience. Even before her accident, Donna had never really felt comfortable in a kitchen. Cooking had never been her strong point or even an interest. Her mother, Jean, was the cook in the family, noted for her wonderful Italian cooking and tasty sauces.

As much as Donna steered away from food preparation more complicated than a fruit salad or a bowl of cereal, she suddenly took a great interest in clipping coupons. Her mother had started sending her coupons and suggested she start clipping, too. Because of her head injury, it was difficult for Donna to determine what she really needed and would actually use. Consequently, she clipped with a passion, cutting out and using almost every coupon that appeared in the paper.

If Donna needed something and didn't see it in plain sight, it never occurred to her to open drawers or cabinets to see if she had any in stock. But she knew for sure that Safeway had it. So armed with fists full of coupons, off to Safeway she would go, loading the cupboards and refrigerator with items she would never ever use, many in duplicate and triplicate. For the bathroom, she had stockpiled a nine-month supply of shampoo and a lifetime supply of contact solution, lipstick and nail polish. It reached such a point that in addition to my "no shopping today" admonitions, I began posting, large friendly reminders on her bulletin board. "*No shopping today,*" they read. At one time, I lovingly referred to her apartment as our Mini-Safeway.

Either Donna didn't see the notices or she failed to retain the message. She had a penchant for navy blue tights. Although she already had an ample supply, she'd buy more each time she went to the store. Something kept telling her, "I need blue tights." In time, she had drawers full of them. She eventually sent a dozen pairs of them to her sister, Carolyn.

All of Donna's spending left her checking account a mess. When Donna went shopping, she had gotten into the habit of paying by check; however, she neglected to record every transaction in her checkbook and she definitely needed help. Since my sister Kathe was an accountant by profession, she decided to try and help Donna straighten out her bookkeeping.

On Thursday evenings, following their dinners together, Kathe would sit with Donna and attempt to fill in the blanks. Retracing her steps during the previous week was often impossible so the time was spent more as a memory exercise. Donna was not always a willing subject. She considered doing bookwork a chore and easily grew impatient with it, as well as growing impatient with my sister.

As Kathe remembered, "Donna would come home from therapy and grumble about having to do juvenile things such as drawing pictures and practicing writing. 'I want to get on with the important things in life,' she'd say. Then we'd start on the bookwork, which was very important because it was helping her become independent. There were times when I had to be very firm with her to get her started. She might want to ride her stationary bike or sort through piles of pictures. She was easily distracted. Once she got on track, however, she was determined not to let paperwork get her down.

She knew she could do it. She just had to keep at it and practice.

"Donna had so much courage. There were times when I'd ask myself, 'What would I do if I were in her shoes?' I honestly don't know if I would have the courage to forge ahead the way she did. Very seldom would she get discouraged."

Donna wasn't discouraged yet, but she was beginning to miss working. She may not have relished doing bookwork, but paperwork was another matter. For her job at Kodak, she often stayed up late working on her accounts. She had loved being organized, writing reports, keeping current. Her strong work habits not only made her a better salesperson, they helped take her to the top. Her inquiry about coming to my office to help out made it obvious she needed an ongoing project to keep her mind stimulated.

What could she do that was creative and involved keeping records? It had to be something she enjoyed, something she would eagerly want to continue day after day and, at the same time, challenge her thinking.

I came up with the idea of keeping a diary. It seemed like the perfect solution. She would have to stretch her memory to recall the events of each day and, if she kept at it, would in time have an invaluable personal record of her recovery. Because of her lack of focus and the challenge of her short-term memory, I didn't know if this would interest her or if she could even do it.

I didn't have long to wait for an answer. When I presented Donna with her first diary, a small fabric-covered book decorated with her favorite teddy bears and tiny hearts, her eyes opened wide and a big smile crossed her face. On the evening of October 2, 1985, she wrote:

Today is the first day I've written in my new diary.
Vinetta and I went for a walk down by the pier

when therapy got over with today. It felt really good walking and then we had dinner. My nails are getting really long and it's great to have them manicured once a week. Mom just called. I'll write more tomorrow.

As the days passed, Donna began to confide more in her diary. Her entries became longer and more detailed. The little book truly became a part of her, and traveled with her wherever she went. According to Vinetta, "She panicked a little if she couldn't find her pen when thoughts came to her. If someone said something she wanted to remember, or if something came to her during the night, she'd get up and write in her diary."

As Roy Noble recalled, "Her diary helped her through the days, and getting through the days was a big problem. She was up so early that she grew tired and bored by the time everyone else's day was just starting."

Writing in her diary was certainly better for Donna than reading a book, which had been recommended to her earlier as a means of helping pass periods of time and frustration. It was difficult for Donna to retain anything. She would read a page or two, put the book down, then forget what she had just read. She also had to use a ruler to guide her along the lines of text on the page, one line at a time. Without the ruler she became too easily distracted. Except for the occasional misplacing of her pen, the diary presented no distractions. She noted some weeks later in her diary:

I write in my diary whenever I have a free moment. I don't have too many of those but if someone's late for one reason or another, I start writing.

Diary, October 15, 1985

An added bonus was a noticeable improvement in Donna's penmanship. She had always prided herself on her neat handwriting. But for months after she came out of her coma, it was virtually illegible. She had what is known as *left avoidance*, a condition which caused her to avoid the left side of things, including the left side of paper as she wrote. For a time, she was only able to print in block letters. However, as her coordination returned, she began to connect letters in a crude form of handwriting. She would begin writing in the middle of the page and her writing would slant extremely up or extremely down. At that point, Rosemary suggested she get a workbook to help her penmanship, but Donna balked. "Forget it," Donna resisted. "I'm not doing that childish stuff. I'll write in my diary." Her handwriting didn't improve immediately, but with each entry she was making progress.

She was also making progress in other areas. She was allowing herself to reach out to others again and resume relationships. After the unfortunate incident with her brother, Jimmy, we felt she might never again want anyone to disrupt her private world. But when she heard that Sue Erickson, her dear friend from Kodak, was coming to town, she insisted that Sue stay with her. Sue and Donna had known each other for years, ever since Donna's days as a trainee with Kodak during her junior year in college. They had kept in touch ever since even though Sue worked out of the Phoenix area. With Donna's transfer to Los Angeles, they were brought together more frequently at regional sales meetings. On those occasions, they even roomed together. Now Donna eagerly awaited being Sue's roommate again, if only for a little while.

It was almost like old times. They laughed, they talked, they exchanged stories about work, clothes and marathon shopping sprees. But around eight o'clock one evening, Donna abruptly said, "My brain is tired.

ONE MORE SUNSET

I'd better let it rest." Without saying another word, she left the room and went to bed.

The next morning Sue awakened to find every drawer and cupboard door wide open. She began to panic, thinking a robber had entered during the night. But it had only been Donna wandering about in the dark, apparently looking for something. Donna didn't remember what she was looking for, but she did explain her disappearance so early the previous evening. "My brain can only last so long," she said, "and I knew I had reached that point. I had to get to bed right away. It didn't matter what was going on after eight o'clock."

Sue understood. She listened patiently as Donna talked about her limitations, even her weight gain and why she only picked at her food. "I am used to her eating habits," said Sue. "When Donna was with Kodak she often skipped meals, and she never took time for lunch. She was much too preoccupied with her work. Now she is even more determined to succeed. It's obvious with everything she attempts. In many ways, she puts me to shame. I was on the stationary bike for 20 minutes and got off exhausted. She was on for 45 minutes, then started all over again. I could hear her saying to herself, 'I'm going to get better. I'm going to get stronger.'"

In October 1985, seven months after the accident, Donna had to use all her reasoning skills to make a decision that had to be hers alone. Her mother had been pressing her to come home to Connecticut for the Christmas holidays. I thought she would jump at the invitation, but it only seemed to agitate and confuse her. She asked me what she should do. Not wanting to put added pressure on her, one way or the other, I told her to think about it. She had plenty of time to make up her mind.

Everyone she asked at the hospital said basically the same thing, "Wait and see." She said she would, but in her diary she wrote:

I don't want to go. I want to stay right here. I like being around people that know where things are and don't ask a lot of questions. I don't even miss anyone from back east except my grandfather. It's weird not to miss anyone, but right now I'm so busy with therapy and working so hard to get back to normal that I really don't have time.

Diary, October 25, 1985

PHOTOS

Donna having fun in the snow on a ski trip at Hunter Mountain, New York, shortly before her transfer to California in 1980.

Donna on a ballooning/ski trip in Aspen, Colorado with Jim Connelly (left), Bob Franks and Lori Hickey, 1983.

Donna costumed as a Kodak camera for Halloween 1985, with friend and driver Wayne Reeder.

The Christina

*July 24, 1985, Kate, Jimmy and Kate's sister Maureen,
abord the yacht "The Christina" the day he
"couldn't afford to fall in love."*

Donna visits with Dr. Barry Ludwig at New Pathways,
one year after the accident, 1986.

Wayne Gretzky invited Donna to a practice session, 1986.

Donna dressed in her Fourth of July outfit for volunteer work at Daniel Freeman Hospital, with Sister Margaret O'Connell, 1986.

Sister Margaret Walsh and Sister Jean O'Leary in the hospital cafeteria, where they met Donna, 1987.

*Donna with one
of her favorite
teddy bears,
1987.*

*Jim Connelly in a happy
moment at Donna's
apartment, 1987.*

*In 1992,
Donna looking
radiant and
confident, working
with Jimmy in
real estate.*

*Jim and his son
Jeff, 1990.*

Donna and Cardinal Mahony in Los Angeles, 1994.

Donna with her friend and mentor, Jim Connelly, 1994.

*Donna and
Katy Clare, 2^1/$_2$,
1994.*

Katy Clare, Kate and Jim Connelly 1994.

Window shopping with Sue Erickson, Donna's good friend from Kodak, 1994.

Donna with her reminder board, 1994.

Jimmy, his mother Clare and Lou Holtz in Los Angeles 1994.

The Lou Holtz philosophy of Commitment, Trust and Love inspired Jimmy to continue with his own commitment to Donna's recovery, September 1999.

*Lou Holtz and Donna together after
Lou's memorable and motivating talk in
Los Angeles 1994.*

Donna enjoys one of the many sunsets in Manhattan Beach, 1995.

Donna parcipates in 10K run through the streets of Manhattan Beach, 1995.

Jim's mother, Clare, and dear friend, Roy Noble, in Donna's apartment, 1998.

Paula Sarcona and Donna relaxing on the beach under the Manhattan Beach Pier, 1998.

*Roy and Betty Noble, two of Donna's guardian angels,
visit with her on her garden patio.*

*Kate, Jimmy and Donna in her alma mater
sweatshirt at the N.D. - Boston College football
game prior to kick-off 1999.*

Donna proudly displays her organized refrigerator!

Donna and her mother, Jean, 1999.

*Donna visits the University of
Notre Dame, 2000.*

CHAPTER 9

Donna on the Loose

Donna did go home for a visit, but not for the holidays. She went several weeks before Christmas. Her decision to visit her family in Connecticut came as a surprise, for every time we discussed the possibility, she became extremely anxious and agitated, waving her arms up and down, back and forth, saying she didn't want to go. Donna wanted to stay in Manhattan Beach where she was familiar with everything and could walk everywhere. But she also missed her family and didn't want to disappoint her mother.

Donna called me several times a day while she was gone. Although she was with her family and Jami, a woman who worked for me and acted as chaperone and companion for Donna throughout the trip, Donna said she felt grounded hearing my voice. It had a calming effect on her, she admitted, especially when things were not going well for her.

Mealtimes were always a problem. Jean spent hours in the kitchen cooking her daughter's favorite Italian dishes, just as Donna liked them, drowning in sauces. At the table, however, Donna stubbornly refused to touch them. Repeatedly, she would say, "You're not going to tempt me, ma. I'm not eating!" So Donna bypassed the specialty items in favor of salads, fruits and vegetables. Even then, she only picked at her food.

Perhaps the meals set the tone for Donna's visit. Jean grew more concerned about her daughter's eating habits with each passing day, and her concern was not always expressed in a supportive way. Donna had lost weight, but it was really nothing to worry about. Not yet, anyway. Before she left on her trip she had been weighed at the hospital. At that point, the scale indicated 124 pounds. Donna was down only three pounds from her high of 127.

What upset Donna more than anything, however, was that her family reacted to her as if she had suddenly become fragile and helpless. "They treat me like I'm retarded," she complained during one of her many phone calls. "They keep telling me, 'Don't do this' and 'Don't do that.' They won't let me do anything."

Donna certainly wasn't fragile, nor was she helpless. She could do whatever she wanted, within reason. It may have taken her a little longer, but she'd get it done—one way or another.

It was my philosophy to let Donna learn by doing. If she had an interest in something, I encouraged her. She may have made mistakes, but on the next try—and the next and the next—she'd be another step ahead.

BE POSITIVE was the everyday motto, in one form or another. It came across in conversations and in written messages that topped Donna's bulletin board. But the positive words weren't only for Donna. They were also intended for everyone who worked closely with her, reminders that a positive attitude was the key to everything we were trying to accomplish. It was permissible to be firm, if necessary, but never negative. I must admit that whenever I let a negative remark slip, either out of frustration or impatience, Donna really took note. My attitude had a strong effect on her and she tried harder to please me so that I would get back to the positive.

In the long run, however, a poor attitude simply does not work. We learned that firsthand from many of Donna's doctors, therapists and counselors, whose attitudes were less than positive. Had we listened to them, we'd have thrown in the towel soon after we started. Because of my unorthodox thinking, I was not one of their favorite people. Thank God for Dr. Ludwig and Rosemary. They were among the few who endorsed our style and remained positive. If it hadn't been for their positive support and enthusiasm, Donna and her team of caregivers, the "A-Team," might not have been able to keep going. As it was, we had to double our efforts when Donna returned from Connecticut.

Knowing how concerned Jean was about her daughter, Clare took the initiative to write Jean a letter. She wanted to reassure Jean by letting her know just how well Donna was doing and that she was improving daily. As the days passed, Donna had forgotten the downside of her visit back home, thanks to her lack of short-term memory. Donna dwelled only on having seen her grandfather again. That, she said, was the highlight of her trip.

Donna's return was only a week or so prior to Christmas, and she was able to keep busy preparing for the holidays. She had plenty to do after being away, such as decorating the house, addressing Christmas cards and coordinating holiday outfits. Surprisingly, for the holidays Donna decided to have her long nails trimmed. On December 18 she wrote:

> I had really long nails that a manicurist just cut back and trimmed. Now it's much easier to do anything with fine motor skills. I will definitely keep them short from now on.

Donna was an avid collector of teddy bears, mostly bought by me when I went on business trips. They all had names and she remembered each and every one. Her favorite was a bear named Joe Montana, which was the first bear I gave her. When she woke up from the coma, I wanted her to have something warm to hold on to so I found this soft, cuddly bear at the hospital in Missoula, Montana. Because I knew Donna identified with winners and because she was in Montana, we named him Joe Montana.

Her teddy bears were on display throughout her apartment. Instead of buying a Christmas tree that first year in Manhattan Beach, she and Vinetta decorated one of the bears. This Christmas bear brought smiles to our faces. As Vinetta remembered, "It was helpful for Donna to work with things she favored. She loved her bears and that kept her interested in what we were doing. She had fun decorating it with ribbons and ornaments. It was wonderful to hear her laugh."

Rosemary suggested that Donna see *The Nutcracker* as part of her holiday celebration. Although it irritated Donna to dress up and put on makeup, she eagerly looked forward to going into Los Angeles to the theater.

Once she got into her seat, however, she saw very little of the production. "It was obvious she wasn't having a good time," Vinetta said. "She started nodding off after only a few minutes and from then on she couldn't keep her head up. The show just wasn't stimulating for her. It was evening, she was tired and she was not directly interacting with the show. These are common behaviors of persons with head injury and we caretakers need to be aware. She was easily agitated and when things started shutting down for her, we would take a break. Changing activities was often the solution, so that night we left well before the show was over." On the evening of December 30, upon her return home from *The Nutcracker*, she wrote in her diary:

> The play was good only if you like ballet. I don't like it so I thought it stunk. All I wanted to do was go to sleep.

Knowing Donna as we did, it was probably naive of us to think she could sit still for a period of time without becoming drowsy, anxious or bored. To keep Donna's interest, she had to be "on the go"—walking, working out on her bike, anything physical, even shopping. However, she avoided clothing stores because she vowed never to buy anything to wear until she was down to a size 5.

She could not read or watch television without falling asleep. The noise of a radio was too distracting and created confusion for her. Writing in her diary was fine for short periods, but it was impossible for her to stay with it for any length of time. She couldn't even stay in bed all night. She continued to be up and down, often up for good as early as 3:00 a.m. to ride her bike.

One morning, she wandered into the living room at 4:30 a.m., turned on all the lights and the television, climbed on her stationary bike, and as she was pedaling away, turned to me, as I was trying to sleep on the sofa, and whispered, "I'm not bothering you, am I?"

Donna was becoming much more independent and we continued to encourage her. We even said yes when she suggested walking around the community on her own. It was a halfhearted yes, but the right thing to say. Only the night before she had commented, "It really irritates me when people try to make decisions *for* me instead of *with* me. They act as though I shouldn't have a say in the matter at all." It wasn't much later she apologized for "the way I often snap at people." But Donna was right; this was a common mistake people made, assuming she was not capable of helping with a decision.

On January 15, nine months after the accident, Donna entered her "Ultimate Goals for 1986" in her diary, which were "to gain 100% recovery" by (1) improving balance, (2) continuing to improve memory, (3) gaining 100% independence, and (4) accepting responsibility by choosing restaurants and making reservations, locking the door and remembering where the key is, and reading the mail. I always told Donna if we don't set our sights high enough, we will never know how far we can reach. Donna was reaching for the stars.

Donna's "Goal Number Four" was bracketed with the notation "already doing these." But "Number Three" was probably highest on her list, especially after her request to walk unsupervised around the neighborhood. Watching her leave that first morning was like having a child go off to school for the first time. But as with a child, we had no intention of letting her strike out completely on her own. Without Donna knowing it, either Vinetta or I followed wherever she went.

To be doubly safe, Donna was loaded with identification and phone numbers taped to everything she wore and carried. There was always the possibility that she could elude us and need our help.

Donna had at least two destinations scheduled each day, and they were always the same: the laundromat and the camera shop. Finding something for her to do until the stores opened wasn't always easy. She was usually up and ready to go three to four hours before they unlocked their doors.

Her daily trips became routine, but they were not without incident. Although she knew where to take her rolls of film to be processed, she didn't always remember where she put them once she took them out of the camera. Many times I'd walk through the front door and find Donna frustrated and angry, furiously looking through drawers and pockets, trying to find her film from the day before. More times than not, she had forgotten that she had already taken it down to be developed.

She was frequently confused about the whereabouts of her laundry, as well. George, who owns the local laundromat, Whale of a Wash, became the target of her temper on more than one occasion when Donna accused him of losing her clothes. It may have been a blouse or a skirt or a dress. Whatever it was, Donna was certain George had misplaced it. "I can't find it anywhere," she would tell him. "It's gone. You lost it!" This went on day after day. Patiently, George would tell Donna to go home and look for the missing items.

"I've already looked," was Donna's reply. "And you know what? Sometimes I get other people's laundry. So you're giving their stuff to me and my stuff to them! And I'm not giving theirs back ever!"

He wasn't really. Donna simply didn't remember some of the items, especially those newly given to her, so she thought they belonged to someone else. As for the "lost" clothes, they were never missing at all. Either Donna had misplaced them or they were still hanging in her closet.

It finally got to the point where George did not want to do business with Donna anymore. Hearing that really upset her. She wrote to George: "For a long time, I have been starting every day by going to Whale of a Wash and talking to you. I want to always be your customer."

The next morning, I delivered the note to George along with a load of Donna's laundry. He took her back as a customer and she stopped accusing him. For weeks afterward, whenever she looked for an item she specifically wanted to wear and couldn't find it, I would hear, "Someone stole that!" It finally got to the point where I told her, jokingly, "The man from Utah came and took it." For a time it seemed that the man from Utah, whoever he was, had taken everything.

This imaginary person became the comic relief when we couldn't find something and together we accused "The man from Utah."

Donna and George resumed their friendship, visiting daily and talking about travel often. George, a native of Argentina, has traveled the world. He is quite interesting and takes time to share stories with Donna. And yes, he is still doing her laundry.

Following Donna from place to place was more than simply keeping an eye on her. We wanted to make sure she waited at stoplights and obeyed traffic signs, that she was headed in the right direction, and that she knew her way home. Early on, her direction was terrible. She got turned around easily and became confused, especially after coming out of a store. But after a time, she learned to recognize various landmarks, such as a billboard, building, or storefront. The westward direction was no problem. She could see the ocean from every street corner.

It took months before I felt confident enough to let Donna venture out on her own. Her first independent walk was down to her landlord's office to pay the rent. It was not far—only about four blocks from her home. But she had to cross a major intersection and make two turns. Miraculously, she made it. Even then I left little to chance. She still carried my name and phone number in her purse and on stickers attached to her clothing. I had drilled into her what to do in case she was lost. "Always look for a policeman or someone in uniform," I told her. "A construction worker is good, too. They are good, dependable people, hard workers who will help you."

Thank heaven she remembered the advice. One morning she left to buy some sweatshirts at Target, which was about 1.5 miles straight east from her apartment. At her pace, the walk should have taken her about 40 minutes. But an hour later and still no Target, she decided to keep walking, determined to find the store.

She was still walking when, miles later, she reached Los Angeles International Airport. She looked for the sun, another instruction I'd given her. "Find the sun and head west," I had said. But that day was overcast with no sun, and as a result, she headed east—the wrong direction.

Unable to spot anything the least bit familiar, and uncertain how to retrace her steps, she kept walking until she found a construction site. Then she asked a worker for directions back to Manhattan Beach.

It wasn't unusual for me to get an "SOS" phone call in the middle of the day. At least two or three times a month I'd receive calls from beach cities down the coast. Donna had walked the bike path that borders the ocean, taking in the scenery until she had lost track of time and her way. Not knowing where she was, she needed a ride home.

She even managed to get lost with Vinetta, her companion, at her side. They were attending the Auto Show at the Convention Center in Los Angeles, and in the crowd they became separated. Donna didn't panic. She simply looked around, first for Vinetta, then for a telephone. By then she had committed my phone number to memory, and she was able to call me herself. On this particular occasion, I called security and had them page Vinetta and Donna to come to the security office where they could be reunited. The real bonus here was the fact that Donna did not lose control and thought things through. She had come such a long, long way.

Being able to venture to more distant areas and find her way home gave Donna ideas. Her job at Kodak had her moving from one location to another, covering up to one hundred miles or more each day. Now she wanted to pick up the pace and expand her territory beyond walking distance. She wanted to get on her bicycle, the one in the garage that wasn't stationary, the one that could take her wherever she wanted to go. She even had her helmet ready.

The request came near the end of Vinetta's service. As much as she wanted to please Donna, she could not recommend the bicycle for her client. "We were afraid to get the bike out at that time," Vinetta remembered, "because Donna had tunnel vision, which blocked her peripheral vision, particularly on her left side.

"Then, too, her direction was so poor. How could she ride a bike without knowing what was going on around her or where she was going?"

Donna took the turndown in stride, probably because she had a backup plan. If she couldn't ride her bicycle, then she could drive a car. "I'll be safer in a car," she reasoned. "And I'm a good driver. I've driven almost all my life."

In her career with Kodak, much of her day was spent driving to visit her customers. While she had put in a lot of miles behind the wheel, she tended to have a heavy foot. In the three years I had known her prior to her head injury, she had a minor traffic accident every year. Nothing serious, mostly fender benders, but it was a real concern. No telling what might have happened next. Besides, I'm overly protective. I couldn't chance having anything else happen to her, not after what she had been through.

Donna had her mind so set on driving that she wouldn't let the subject drop. My explanation seemed to make no sense to her. Either that or she just refused to accept it. But I would not give in. For the time being, the best I could tell her was "not right now" and "let's wait and see." However, that wasn't good enough for Donna. "You can be afraid of anything if you let yourself be," she said, firing back. It got to the point that any talk of driving became a sore spot between us.

To help ease the tension, I wrote her a poem.

A winner to me is easy to see.
Lover of life, not into strife.
Paying her dues so not to lose.
Respected by all so never to fall.
Donna's the one, she makes it fun.

146

The poem helped a little, but the pending arrival of her mother caused her to turn her thoughts away from driving and more toward her mom's visit. I was concerned that the visit would be extremely stressful for Donna. In the months Donna had been home since her pre-Christmas visit to Connecticut, she had mentioned nothing about her encounters with her family. Now I feared the questions about her eating, weight loss, and more would start all over again.

Donna had lost quite a few pounds since Christmas, and while she liked the way she looked, she wasn't happy about her decreased stamina. She grew tired easily, and with Dilantin no longer to blame, she believed her diet was partly responsible. Slowly, cautiously, she was beginning to expand her menu.

I just woke up and its 2:35 a.m. Mom's sound asleep (like most people at this hour). I'm a little bit hungry now but nothing that can't wait a while. Jami and Mom were saying I'm getting too skinny. I haven't even weighed myself since I weighed 111 pounds and took size 5. All the size 5 clothes Jami just got me are too big for me now. That's a riot. I can't believe size 5 is too big. I've never been this thin. I love it! All I'm doing is eating foods that are nutritious, like chicken, fish, a lot of fruit. Before I would eat a donut. Now I have an orange.

Diary, March 29, 1986

It's amazing that now everyone is saying to gain weight. Earlier they were saying to lose weight. Jimmy asked if I was going to keep handling it my own way and I said yes. I know I'm eating right so I'll just let my body choose a good balancing weight.

Diary, March 30, 1986

I've been so tired all week and this a.m., upon wak-
ing I felt energized. I hope it had to do with those
eggs last night. I had an omelet for dinner and it
was fantastic! I haven't had one since before the
accident, so I went a whole year without an omelet.
Clare and I were talking about how I haven't had
any red meat (iron) and how my system must be
low on iron. I need to eat meat, eggs and cottage
cheese. If I eat something with those things in it I'm
sure I'll be less tired. It's so exciting that the reason
I'm always so tired is as simple as eating some pro-
tein. I've really cut out so many foods and gone real
heavy into fruit. What I need is more balance.

Diary, April 4, 1986

It may have been Donna's new interest in eating
that led to a wonderful visit with Jean. "She's so
sweet," Donna said of her mother. They seemed to really enjoy each other's company. They took long walks
together, they cleaned closets, and they spent hours in
the kitchen as Jean prepared Donna's favorite meals.
"No one organizes like my mother. She has such great
energy. . . she wears me out!" says Donna. "People ask
me, 'How did you get to be over 30 years old and never
learn to cook?' No problem. Have Mom over once or
twice a year and eat out the rest of the time."

After Jean's visit, Donna went back to visit some
of her new friends at the hospital. One of her therapists
had suggested that she do volunteer work by visiting
patients as part of her therapy. On first hearing, it
sounded like a good idea. Donna was such a people
person. She loved to talk, and she had a ready smile for
everyone she met.

But as the suggestion began to sink in, the idea
enraged her. "More therapy!" she ranted at me. "I'm
fed up with everyone telling me what to do!" She had
been in therapy for ten months and she was rebelling.

During her mother's visit, Donna had gleefully missed several weeks of sessions. Now it was time for her to go again. "I'm trying to cut down on my time at the hospital," she told me, "not add to it. I only have to go back when *I'm* ready to go!"

Often Donna would respond vehemently or negatively to an idea or suggestion upon first hearing it, only to change her mind in a few days or sometimes even a few hours. This was due to the fact that it took her longer to process the information once she received it. This mental behavior is known as *delayed processing* and is very common among head-injured people.

In this instance, a few days later, she was ready not only to resume her therapy sessions but also to give volunteer work a try. Donna took to it immediately. Although she frequently became lost in the maze of hospital corridors, she had great fun wandering about with her camera and delivering flowers and messages. She was asked to stay with the patients only a few minutes, but she always stayed longer, often for hours, gabbing with her new friends. She especially liked the elderly. She even dressed for the occasions. "No one likes being in the hospital on a holiday," she said, "and I want to make them happy." Her red, white and blue Fourth of July outfit was a huge success with the patients and nurses alike.

Donna made two very special friends one day in the hospital cafeteria. Unable to balance her camera, purse and other items along with her tray as she moved through the food line, she looked for a place to put her belongings. It had to be safe because she had a constant fear of her things being stolen, lost or misplaced. That was when she spotted two women sitting alone at a table. Wearing short veils, trailing from their heads to their shoulders, they appeared to be nuns. She went over to their table and introduced herself. "I'm Donna Jones," she said with a smile.

"I'm Sister Jean O'Leary," replied one of the women, "and this is Sister Margaret Walsh." They invited Donna to join them. Donna explained her predicament, went off to get her lunch, and returned with her tray loaded with food. "Doesn't all this look great?" she asked. She took one bite of this, one bite of that, and she was finished.

"Donna really wasn't interested in eating," said Sister Jean. "She wanted only to talk, and she talked the time away. She wound up taking her lunch home with her."

Later that afternoon, Donna enthusiastically told me about her chance meeting with the Sisters. "They're like saints," she said. "They're so beautiful, so inspirational and they're Irish too! They make you feel alive." Then she added, "I told them I begged God to give me happiness and Sister Margaret said 'God doesn't give happiness, He gives blessings. We make our own happiness.'"

From then on, Donna, Sister Jean and Sister Margaret met every Tuesday and Thursday for lunch, each time Donna went to the hospital for volunteer work. When I was able, I joined them. As Donna remarked more than once, being with the Sisters was "the best part of going to the hospital."

On special occasions, they spent time together outside of Daniel Freeman Hospital—luncheons whenever Donna's mother or sister came to visit and various celebrations at the Sisters of St. Joseph's convent. A time most significant was her speaking engagement at the Carondelet Center in Brentwood. Donna took the podium that evening and told an audience of retired Sisters about her travels. "We so admired Donna's determination and enthusiasm," said Sister Margaret. "There were times when she would get lost in the hallways, but she never gave up, even in her confusion. Of course, she always had her camera with her. The pictures she took were invaluable to her. They helped her to remember."

"She'd get so excited," said Sister Jean. "The more excited she became the faster she talked and the higher her voice would get. She was very nasal too, which made her difficult to understand at times. Every so often we would have to remind her to slow down." Donna also had occasional mood swings, the Sisters agreed. "But that was understandable," said Sister Jean.

One subject that really excited Donna was driving. She told the nuns about wanting to drive, and how easy it would be for her to get from Manhattan Beach to the hospital. "I'd never get lost," she told them, "because I've memorized the streets to take. It's simple . . . H . . . I . . . P. That stands for Highland-Imperial-Prairie.

Donna was so proud of a personal note she received from her new friends, the nuns. It read: "You are becoming a great conversationalist."

With her volunteer work and luncheons with Sister Jean and Sister Margaret, Donna was no longer traumatized by the thought of frequent visits to the hospital. She couldn't drive herself there, but that was becoming less and less important to her. What mattered most was planning her day around the good times she would have once she arrived.

Her mood became even brighter with the news that Dr. Ludwig had authorized her transfer to the New Pathways Program, a unit at Daniel Freeman Hospital for advanced head injury treatment. "All your hard work is paying off," I told her. "You're on your way to the graduate school of head injury."

Donna was thrilled. "It's New Pathways here I come," she said, beaming. But her enthusiasm soon gave way to concern. She felt the new program might be overwhelming. She feared the unknown. Would she like the new counselors and therapists? What about the people in her group sessions? Would they ask questions she couldn't answer? Would it be too much, too confusing? I held her close and looked into her eyes and said, "You won't be going through those doors alone, Donna," I assured her. "I'll be there with you as long as you need me."

As it turned out, she didn't need me long at all. Our first meeting with the director of New Pathways was a positive experience. She looked into Donna's eyes, smiled and said, "Someone is home in there." Her words made Donna smile, and clouded my eyes with tears of joy.

It wasn't long before Donna became the top performer in the program, which involved not only life skills, but also fun things like taking field trips and putting on plays. Her progress was amazing, partly because she genuinely enjoyed her sessions, especially the cognitive group, which had her actively participating in the "name game" competitions, e.g., name the state capital, name the flower, animal, etc. The rest was due to her stubborn determination. As was typical of Donna, she simply made up her mind to be the best and not to fail. There were even times when she unknowingly found herself taking on the role of therapist. It was not unusual for her to chime in when others stumbled during a spelling exercise with uplifting comments. "Don't get down on yourself," she would say. "You're doing great. Just give yourself time and you'll get through it."

She displayed incredible strength and compassion. But she would need more than that in the days to come. The most difficult times were ahead, not only for Donna but for everyone else involved in her recovery.

CHAPTER 10

"I Will Not Leave You!"

Kate was now back in California. We had kept in close touch over the months since our chance meeting aboard the yacht following Donna's accident one year ago. Actually, it had been more than keeping "in touch." Driven by her parting words to let her know that "I was thinking about her" enough for her to return, I became relentless in courting her cross-country. After all the messages, phone calls and flowers, how could she not know that I cared more than enough?

She first returned for one short visit, then another. Over the coming year she traveled back and forth a number of times until, at last, she decided to stay. Throughout my pursuit of Kate I had never once mentioned her name to Donna. There were times when I had considered telling Donna only to decide against it. For one thing, during Kate's visits I had no guarantee that our relationship would grow to the point of where she wanted to stay. Another even more important reason was that Donna had enough to think about. Why create added and unnecessary stress and confusion for her? Throughout this time Donna was experiencing periods of great emotional highs and lows. She was thrilled to be doing so well at New Pathways, and she loved the freedom of being able to wander around the community unchaperoned. However, with this freedom came a new awareness, not only of the people and places around her, but of herself. In one way, this was a giant step forward. In another, it created even more problems for her.

By now Donna had become a familiar face along the streets of Manhattan Beach and in the shops and restaurants. Almost everyone who lived or worked there recognized her and knew her name. She had a smile for friends and strangers alike. It seemed to take her forever to walk only a block or two because she would stop to talk to anyone. She loved it when people were interested enough in her to ask questions, especially about the accident and how it happened. It wasn't very long ago that she wouldn't even admit to having an accident, let alone be willing to talk about it eagerly. She answered all questions as honestly as she could, then asked a few herself. She didn't always remember the answers, or with whom she had been talking when she returned home, but something was beginning to click in her mind. These people, almost without exception, were doing things and going places. They had jobs and responsibilities to fill their days. They had more to do than wonder, shop and chat.

Occasionally, she would see people glancing at her oddly or looking back to follow her slightly off-balance gait. She didn't have to mention those moments to me because the quizzical and sometimes stares of pity happened often enough for me to notice whenever we walked together. Sometimes people made remarks about Donna's slurred speech, in question of her sobriety, and we were always concerned that she might be embarrassed at new social occasions. She wasn't drunk, of course, as anyone who knew her was aware.

There had been a time, months earlier, when Donna would have ignored the stares and comments. Now her eyes and ears were becoming increasingly sensitive to all that was taking place around her.

Hearing those negative comments made Donna extremely uncomfortable. She just wanted to hide.

Throughout much of her life, Donna had been the center of attention. Her warm personality, joyous spirit and competitive nature and positive attitude attracted people to her. It was different now. She still felt those things inside but now she was subdued, she didn't want to stand out. Suddenly she wanted to be like everyone else, to function as they did. Until the accident, nothing had ever been impossible for her. Now she was like a boxer with her hands tied, and she became angry. She wanted so desperately to get better, but in her mind all she could see was what she couldn't do. "Good things can happen when you're patient," I reminded her. "I know you're getting tired of hearing that, but it's true. You've come so far and I'm so proud of you."

I meant every word, but it didn't seem to matter. For the first time since I'd known Donna, I saw a negative attitude. Angry about the present and unsure of her future, she was developing a defeatist outlook. "Why me?" she would ask.

"Why did this damn accident happen to me?" She had been through difficult times before, but I'd never known her to have an ounce of quit in her. Until now, it had been possible to inspire her. But with her increasing awareness, she was beginning to turn inward, wanting to shut herself off from the world.

Being aware of this, I started my day by filling up her self-esteem tank for a full hour every morning. This consisted of giving her my complete and undivided attention and reviewing with her all the hard-to-measure progress she had made. We recounted all of her accomplishments since the accident because she was unable to remember them or the good feelings that go along with triumphs. We looked at dozens of photos to help her remember all the interesting people she had met and the fun places she'd been. I'd also have her write me a note to show how her handwriting had improved. I'd have her walk me to some specific location without help from me, to show her she could find her way and that her sense of direction was improving every day. I hoped all of this would build her self confidence. I re-emphasized that she was a valuable person, who made a contribution daily, and that people were learning from her because she was an inspiration. After all the repetition, the coaching and enthusiasm, often times my tank was empty, leaving me exhausted.

It was so unlike Donna to become reclusive, but it was happening. "I didn't want to do anything on my own," she wrote in her diary, "but now I want more time to myself. I really look forward to being alone, away from everything and everyone." Everything truly important to her had always been outside her apartment walls. Now she was confining herself within four very compact walls.

Worried that she was alone too much, I encouraged friends to drop in or call whenever possible. And, without fail, I made it a point to see her daily, in the morning and especially after work and on weekends for our walks. But was it for Donna or for me that our walks to the end of the pier at dusk became so very important? One more sunset, I kept telling myself. One more sunset.

Our walks had always been a time to catch up on our daily activities, her time to unwind. I was also Sears complaint department and let her air all her grievances. Lately, however, Donna wasn't quite so talkative. She was saying less and her voice lacked its usual enthusiasm. The only subject that ignited a spark was work. She desperately wanted to return to Kodak and bury herself in her old job. How could I tell her that was impossible, for the present at least? "Wait and see" had become meaningless.

"I can understand why people commit suicide," she said darkly one early evening, staring out at the open waters of the bay. "I hate to wake up every morning with nothing to do."

Donna seemed to be sinking lower and lower, and my heart was breaking for her. The sad irony was that had she not been improving, she never would have gone through such pain. Her improvement was a double-edged sword. On the positive side, she was becoming more independent; on the negative side she became painfully aware of her limitations. I held her in my arms and said, "We'll figure something out." Then I promised to talk with her therapists the next day.

The therapists and I were often at odds over Donna's therapy. I was progressive and positive; they were not. They wanted Donna to "accept the accident and her limitations" instead of trying to rise above them and do better. I told Donna she could do whatever she wanted to do. She could accomplish anything. They even told me I should stop creating false hopes for Donna and let her live in the present reality of her limitations. My belief was to look to the future with hope and anticipation of an independent life for her. Only God knows what her limitations are. More than one therapist went so far as to tell Donna she should consider the possibility of never getting better and adjust her expectations to less than what I truly believed was possible. I vehemently disagreed with their negative approach to therapy. This time was no exception. My suggestion that they consider a supervised work schedule for Donna met with a negative response. Her depression elicited no sympathy. Depression was not unusual, I was told. It was, in fact, to be expected.

So was their attitude. I took their words as a challenge and replied, "Then I'll take her to work with me." "I guess all the decisions have been made," replied one of the doctors sarcastically, forcing a smile. "Not all the decisions," I answered. "Just the good ones."

Once again I had managed to antagonize people far more experienced than I by letting my heart, rather than my head, guide my decision-making. I honestly believed I knew better than anyone what was best for Donna—what helped her and what didn't, what motivated her and what pulled her down. Except for her emotional distress, she was doing far better than anyone had predicted. How would she be if I hadn't brought her back to California? Still institutionalized in Connecticut, I felt absolutely sure. Even though I didn't have the hospital's blessing or cooperation with the move, I knew in my heart that it was the right thing to do.

The more I thought about my confrontation with Donna's therapists, the better I felt. As long as she wanted to get back into the workplace, and she did with all her heart, I certainly couldn't send her into strange surroundings where she might be confused, embarrassed or even insulted. Only days earlier I had watched the Special Olympics on television. I saw a boy with a voice problem whose therapists had urged him to step out from his sheltered existence into the real world. He did only to be ridiculed by an uncaring stranger. It was months before the boy talked again.

I couldn't chance Donna having a similar experience. As much as I wanted to give her free reign, I found myself still protecting her.

On the morning of December 10, 1986, I drove Donna to my office. As we made our way to the parking lot, I offered a few last minute pointers. "Keep a good attitude," I suggested. "Have an open mind, and try not to be defensive when people ask questions."

"No problem," Donna agreed, smiling. She was so excited, and eager to get started. "This is preparing me for my return to Kodak."

That evening she wrote in her diary:

My first day at the office. I loved it. Barbara Bennetts, in personnel, helped me get acquainted and showed me where to find everyone's desk on a map she'd made. Had trouble remembering the name of one girl, Linda. She didn't look like a Linda to me, so I thought of an association. Every time I saw her I thought of a girl I knew in high school named Linda Farmer. It worked real well. The next time I saw her I said, 'Hi, Linda.' She was impressed. Barbara was so good. She had a list of things for me to do. Here are some of my duties: Fill out a payroll time card and open all the incoming mail . . . Stamp each piece and sort it into separate envelopes for Jimmy, Brenda and Teresa. Ericka had me follow her to the copy room where I copied various pieces of mail and things for Brenda. Started alphabetizing and typing the office Rolodex (a real project), then got water out of the Sparklets machine and distributed the mail. Got lost a couple of times, which was OK. Even with the map I had a hard time finding the restroom, but I made it. Brought my diary but I was much too busy to write in it. This isn't like therapy where it's boring and I have plenty of extra time to write.

Diary, December 10, 1986

Although Donna worked only two days a week, sandwiched between her sessions at New Pathways, she looked like a full-time executive. She carried a briefcase, stuffed with magazines and her diary, and she dressed to the hilt. After wearing casual clothes, mainly sweats, for well over a year, she admitted it was a real pleasure for her to wear "good outfits." Ordinarily, she didn't like to dress up. Now she found it to be fun. She had a reason to pull out clothes that had been hanging unused for much too long. While it was a challenge for Donna to coordinate a new outfit each work day, she did a great job and I was proud of her. We all were. After Donna's first few days, my mother, Clare, wrote her a note: "Hope you are enjoying going to the office. Everyone says you are doing very well. Keep up the good work!" Donna treasured Clare's words. She taped the note in her diary.

On the days when I was unable to drive Donna to the office, Roy, Jami or one of my cousins, Tony, or Josh, filled in for me. After a time, however, Donna felt capable of getting there on her own. Luckily, she could take a bus running through Manhattan Beach and transfer to another that would take her close enough to the office. Donna's first few trips by herself had me fidgeting. She was successful, but it was no accident. I choreographed it as carefully as any professional dancer might choreograph a new dance—step by step.

Before Donna's first solo trip, I introduced myself to the bus driver, Ron, and explained Donna's remarkable recovery. I then gave him $10.00 and asked him to make sure she got off at the right stop. Then, without her knowing it, I followed her to the bus bench to make certain she waited at the right corner and took the right bus. She didn't miss a beat, making her way like a veteran commuter. But she was still having a problem with her peripheral vision. Several times I sneaked up and sat beside her as she waited for the bus to arrive. On one particular morning I started coughing to get her attention. She finally turned and said, "Oh, it's you, Jimmy. When I got home tonight I was going to tell you about this crazy guy sitting next to me who kept coughing."

On a number of occasions, I even followed her bus in my car to make sure she made the right connections. Several times I would drive ahead, park my car, then hide in the coffee shop across the street from where she got off the bus. I would then walk behind her about 50 feet as she walked the last six blocks to work. That whole experience of commuting by herself was one of the best confidence builders for Donna. However, she still had to work through the pain of losing her independence, unable to drive, and now having to take the bus.

Donna's days at the office seemed to revitalize her. Having a place to go and a reason to get dressed up made her happy. Her favorite activity was socializing with the other employees, and she did that extremely well. Although she was doing a commendable job, her primary accomplishment was in acquiring a new sense of self-worth. I called her "the comeback kid."

That Christmas of '86 Donna wrote me a note: "Your support and love throughout my rehabilitation have been second to none. Knowing that you are there makes each obstacle that much easier to bear. We have become so close and have shared so much. I appreciate and thank you for your immense help and guidance, more than I can ever say. You are simply the best. I love you for life."

It was a beautiful note, reflecting her immense appreciation but also her strong dependence. It was several months later in early 1987 that Donna and I faced one of the biggest challenges of our relationship. During a business meeting at the Marina City Club, Donna saw Kate for the first time. I was conducting an evening seminar called "The Power of Goal-Setting" and Kate was assisting me. Donna had heard me talking so much about the seminar that she wanted to attend. I was happy to have her there. Her smiling face told me she was happy, too. It was something different for her to do and she actually was an integral part of my presentation. I told Donna's story as an example of the success of goal-setting. When I noticed half of the audience was in tears and appeared very distraught, I said, "No, no, this has a happy ending." I then introduced Donna to a standing ovation.

Later that evening, I drove Donna back to her apartment in Manhattan Beach. We were discussing the seminar when suddenly she asked, "Who was that lady helping you?"

"That was Kate," I answered. "Her name is Kate Kelly."

"She's a lovely person," said Donna, "and quite sophisticated. Does she have a boyfriend?"

I didn't know what to say. We had always been honest with each other and I wanted to continue to be, but perhaps this wasn't the right time to tell Donna about my relationship with Kate. I kept hoping that she would recover to the point where logic would set in and she would understand. Was she strong enough and independent enough to accept the truth now? The moment I had been dreading had finally arrived. "Yes," I confessed. "She has a boyfriend," and after a long pause I said, "It's me." I had given Kate a ring. We were engaged. I wanted to tell Donna but I couldn't. I was already sick to my stomach as those few words came out.

Donna was silent for a long moment, staring out the car window as we drove back toward Manhattan Beach. When she finally spoke her voice was barely audible. It was difficult to tell if she was talking to me or to herself. "Who will be with me?" she asked. "Who will I talk to?"

"I'll be here," I answered. "I'm not going to leave you."

"Don't you have to be with Kate?"

"I won't abandon you, Donna. I met Kate nearly three years ago and I'm still here. I'll be with you three years from now and three years after that and three years after that. Nothing's going to change. If anything, things will get better."

"Are you allowed to be seen with me?"

"Of course."

"How can you get away with that?" I could hardly keep my composure as I held back the tears, feeling her fear of being abandoned. Her questions reminded me of someone in the eighth grade, afraid of losing her favorite boyfriend. When you lose your boyfriend in the eighth grade, you're not allowed to talk to him because his new girlfriend won't permit it. That was the emotional level at which she was operating, and I wanted so much for her to believe that she would be in my life forever.

"Kate understands," I said. "A very dear friend of hers was in a serious accident, too. She fully understands my commitment to you. And she is not a jealous person."

"But you were *my* friend."

"I *am* your friend. I always will be. Nothing will change." She sank into deep silence again. What more could I say to convince her?

"You always fixed things for me," she said, at last, "but you can't fix this. Maybe I should have died."

I could feel the fear and confusion racing through her. So many questions. So many frightened comments. I put my hand on hers and she began to cry. We were both crying as we pulled up to her apartment. I stayed with her till she was calm, tucked her in and told her I'd see her in the morning.

When I got back to my apartment, Kate was waiting for me. I must have looked very sad because she knew right away what had happened and she came over and hugged me.

We were both sad and relieved at the same time. Our relationship was now out in the open, but we didn't know what long-term effects it would have on Donna.

I was back at Donna's the next morning at 5:00 a.m. She was in the kitchen fixing her breakfast, a bowl of cereal and some fruit. "Would you like some?" she offered. There was a sadness in her voice.

"Sounds good," I replied. We sat together, barely eating, searching for the right words to say, not wanting to hurt one another. Over and over I told her that I wasn't abandoning her. I had to make that clear, that nothing would change.

It had always been my intention to help Donna get better. Few people understood my involvement, however. They would ask, even in front of Donna, "Why are you doing this? What's in it for you?" Nothing was in it for me except increasing the meaning of my life and the opportunity to help someone who was precious to me. I'd had a successful, wonderful life, freedom, financial security and all that goes with it. But no one else was stepping up to the plate. That was made clear to me in Montana and even clearer at Yale-New Haven Hospital. It was as simple as that. No one stepped forward to take charge. No one was willing to interrupt their life to help her. And because I felt Donna deserved the best fighting chance possible, I chose to help her and my life changed dramatically.

As Donna and I sat at the breakfast table, she didn't sound or appear angry, only lost. It would have been so easy for her to say, "Jimmy, I hate you" or "I want you to go" or "Get out!" In spite of everything that had happened, and her mind must have been in turmoil, she never lashed out at me. She never was mean or hurtful. As painful as it must have been for Donna, I had the feeling she was really trying to adjust to the situation.

How would I have reacted had I been in her place? I had been the most important person in her life for the past six years. I had always been there for her, always available to her. We were together through good times and bad, and that is the way it would always be. She may have wanted to hate me, but perhaps deep down she knew that wasn't in her best interest. No matter how dark her thoughts were from time to time, Donna was a fighter and a survivor. As my mother had said soon after the accident, "If she wakes up, she'll make it." I was counting on that now more than ever.

Under the circumstances, I felt I shouldn't leave Donna alone for the day. It was Saturday. It was unusual but she had nothing scheduled on her bulletin board. No, I couldn't leave her with nothing to do. She needs to be active, to have fun. "Want to go for a swim?" I asked. She perked up immediately and we took a swim in the ocean.

Donna loved to swim, and she was an excellent swimmer. We learned, however, that she became disoriented in the ocean. It was too rough for her, especially with the undertow. I had first introduced her to the pool at the Marina City Club in January 1986. Donna was tireless in the water and often put other swimmers to shame, both in distance and speed. It wasn't unusual to see her swim lap after lap, racking up one hundred or more, get out, towel off, then jump back in again. As she did with the stationary bike, she would forget what she had been doing only minutes earlier.

As careful as Donna was in the pool, she frequently surfaced with raw knuckles and fingertips, especially early on at the Club pool. Unable to judge the distance between laps, she continually scraped her hands against the pool walls. She was as surprised as anyone to see the sorry condition of her bruised fingers. In the water or out, she was never aware of any pain, she told me. And so she kept hitting the walls. At that point, her fingers had to be taped whenever she went in the water to keep her from hurting herself even more. She readily admitted that she enjoyed the special attention from me as I taped each of her fingers individually.

Often her brain did not register pain or exhaustion. She would take such long walks that blisters formed on her feet and she didn't know it until she removed her shoes and saw the raw skin.

I remember vividly the time she came over to our house at 5 o'clock in the morning holding her hand up, blood dripping everywhere. I wrapped her hand in a towel and covered it with a plastic bag. Seeing this deep cut sent shivers down my spine and realizing she was not in pain or aware of the seriousness of this injury was another reminder of her need for constant supervision.

One week had passed since I told Donna about Kate. On that day I drove Donna to the Marina City Club pool after breakfast and she had a surprise encounter. At 4:00 that afternoon, Kate arrived to join her sister, Maureen, who had been lounging poolside. I told Kate that I would drop Donna off and perhaps this would be a good time for the two of them to spend some time together. Donna didn't know Maureen, but she recognized Kate from the seminar, and soon the two women were talking. Kate later admitted to being nervous about meeting Donna, not knowing how Donna would receive her. But Donna was characteristically warm and gracious. Even the sight of Kate's engagement ring elicited only congratulatory remarks. Donna's restrained behavior made the chance meeting considerably easier for Kate. Had I been there as well, the atmosphere might have been different, possibly emotional or charged with tension. Their visit was more positive than we expected.

It's true that when things upset or displeased Donna, she could become highly excitable. She would sometimes go into this uncontrollable rage, that we later and lovingly dubbed the "Michael Jackson dance." With her face all red and jaw locked, she would bounce on her toes and verbalize very loudly what was on her mind, all the while moving her arms in very precise, very sharp, quick movements that looked like she was directing traffic in fast forward. She didn't care if she were in a private or public place. On more than one occasion, I was afraid she would have a stroke. As quickly as these fits would start, oftentimes a simple "calm down" would settle her.

It's also true that she had a way of blocking out situations or events that caused her pain. She had become quite good at "blocking out" since the accident. But, then, she probably always had been good at that. Perhaps a part of her early success in sales came from the ability to block out rejection. No doubt, her drive, positive attitude and tremendous determination to succeed during this most critical time in her life were dividends, as well. It all worked together to allow her to keep going.

On my way to see Donna that evening, I had mixed emotions. I was anxious to see her now that she and Kate had actually met. But I was also apprehensive. Would our time together be as emotional as it had been earlier? Would she be angry with me? Was she putting on an act for Kate—or did she genuinely like her?

It was easy to see that something was wrong when I arrived at Donna's apartment. She didn't hurry to greet me. There was no welcome smile or big hello. She appeared lifeless as she sat quietly against the big pillows that lined her sofa. But it wasn't for herself that she seemed so downcast. "I'm sorry I was so rough on you," she said, quietly. "I didn't mean to hurt you."

"I'm fine," I said, sitting beside her.

"This should be a happy time for you and Kate. You have a lot of love to give and Kate's beautiful."

"Kate was very impressed with you. She told me she's never had heroes in life. She does now . . . since she met you."

"Oh, thanks," Donna said. She started to smile, then became downcast again.

"I've been thinking about going home for a visit. I need some hugs and kisses, and Mom's cooking."

"That would be good for you," I said, checking my watch. It was too late to call Connecticut at that point to alert Jean, so I suggested we try in the morning. I wasn't putting off Donna's idea. It was three hours later on the East Coast. There was also a good chance Donna would change her mind by morning or else have completely forgotten about wanting to go. She turned to look out the window. The sun was just beginning to disappear on the horizon. I could tell she was too tired to think about it anymore.

When I arrived at Donna's apartment early the next morning she still had the trip on her mind. Now she wanted to make two calls. She first talked to her best friend, Barbara, who was thrilled to hear Donna would soon be back in Connecticut. She made the second call in high spirits. But I could see her mood sink as the minutes wore on. "What's the problem, Jean?" I asked, taking the phone. It was not a good time for Donna to come home, Jean told me. She was working, Donna's sister was on vacation, one of her brothers was away and the other brother wasn't feeling well. "You've got to pick it up, Jean," I said. "Donna really needs to be with you."

It was no use. To everything I said, and I was pretty rough on her, Jean had an excuse. Maybe the call had come at a bad moment. Maybe the situation in Connecticut wasn't ideal. Well, it wasn't so hot in

California either. I needed to hear a positive word, some willingness to help make things better for Donna during this stressful time, but no adjustments were forthcoming. Maybe Jean was apprehensive or afraid and feeling overwhelmed, but Donna needed her and I needed some help.

As I put the phone slowly back on its cradle, Donna was watching me. "I keep looking for something I'm never going to get when I call home," she said. Her voice was wavering. "I would like my mother to be excited and happy to hear I want to be with her." Donna began to cry as she said, "I would like some happiness in my life." I moved quickly to her side and put my arms around her. It was not the hug she craved from her mother, but I wanted her to know that she was safe, and that I deeply cared about her.

From the time Donna had progressed enough to walk around on her own, she had said, "The minute I'm better, I'm out of here." I loved the determination in her voice and her eagerness to be independent, but I never really took her too seriously. Now she was about to make good her promise—if not to me then to herself. If she couldn't go to Connecticut, she was determined to go someplace else.

In October of 1988, Donna walked into a local travel agency, and they unknowingly encouraged her to take a trip. It seemed a good idea to Donna and that evening she announced to me that she was going to a Club Med resort in Guaymas, Mexico. My first reaction was to say, "No, absolutely not," but knowing how desperately she wanted to get away, I said nothing. Still, I couldn't help but worry. The thought of her going across the country was bad enough. Now she was preparing to go to a foreign land. She confided in her diary:

> I'm feeling depressed. I hope this trip will help my spirits. I really feel the need to go someplace and

meet other people. I feel stuck here and very lonely
now. I'm more in touch with my feelings every day.

Diary, October 10, 1988

Was I wrong in not telling Donna about Kate from the start? It was a question I asked myself often. Since their meeting at the Marina City Club pool, they had seen one another off and on. Now, as Donna anxiously prepared to leave, they spent many hours together. Kate took Donna shopping for bathing suits, coordinated her outfits, and helped her pack. Packing was very stressful for Donna because she couldn't remember what she packed from one moment to the next. She was constantly double-checking to see if she had everything, especially items like her contacts, Laszlo creams and nail products. Afraid she would forget something, she would usually end up with three of everything and her suitcase would be extremely heavy and unmanageable. Kate was a master at packing. What could have taken Donna many hours and been a great source of frustration, Kate made fun, and together they were able to get the job done in less than half an hour. She even helped Donna with her bills so she wouldn't miss a payment while she was away. It made me feel good to see that they were becoming friends.

My stomach was in knots as I drove Donna to the airport and watched her disappear into the plane. I made special requests of the airlines, advising them of her challenges, making them aware of her seat number and asking them to be alert to any help she might need—all without Donna having knowledge of my involvement. I called the manager at the hotel and had him assign an employee to monitor her for safety.

"Let go," I told myself. "Let go! She'll be fine." She was, for the first few days anyway. Then, I got a phone call from her to tell me she was coming back early. She felt really uncomfortable, she said, having to remember all the scheduled activities and where they were taking place.

I was supposed to play tennis at 9:00 a.m. It's 9:50 now and I just finished breakfast. Everything is on a late European schedule here. I'm so confused.

Diary, October 14, 1988

Met a super nice couple, Sally, and her boyfriend, Bud, at the pool. They're going to help me set up a good program of things to do tomorrow. I always have to leave early to do things because I get so lost going places. Was supposed to meet Sally and Bud at their room but couldn't remember the number. I get so frustrated because when I ask for help the people don't speak English. Now that I can tolerate the sound of a radio, it seems so quiet in my room. There's not a TV or anything.

Diary, October 15, 1988

At lunch I forgot where I was sitting or even who I was sitting with when I came back from the restroom. Then I forgot where I put my sunglasses at the pool. The pool is an odd shape, not rectangle or a square, so I couldn't think of them being in a certain place. That about did it. I just called Jimmy to tell him I'm leaving tomorrow. I gave it a good chance and stayed longer than I should have to see if I could handle it, but I can't. With this short-term memory problem I get things very confused and it's too frustrating. I know forgetting is a normal part of life but I always see it as a reminder of the accident. Some vacation! It's been pure torture. I just want to go home where things are familiar to me.

Diary, October 16, 1988

On Donna's return, she jumped back into her old routine with renewed energy. After her experience in Mexico, she was determined to improve her short-term memory. Her therapist at New Pathways had her working on the more remote countries and capitals of the world and she was getting high marks. Her lessons didn't stop there, however. She was now taking advanced swimming lessons at the pool and learning how to operate a computer at home. In a weak moment, I had also agreed to let her take driving lessons. I was still against her driving on her own, but I knew the time was coming when I couldn't stop her, and she had to be prepared. My approval came one evening while we were walking along the streets of Manhattan Beach discussing her progress to date. I had to agree that it far exceeded the expectations of everyone involved in her recovery.

> *Following dinner tonight, Jimmy and I talked about how fast I am coming along. We both feel the finish line is in sight. As I continue to run in that direction, I am so much more aware of the devastation that came with the accident. Although I'm doing well—ahead of schedule—I still feel frustration, anxiety, anger and depression. My next immediate goal is to complete the driving program so I can get behind the wheel of an automobile and be free and independent, and not have to rely on inconveniencing friends and loved ones when I have the urge to change my plans.*

Diary, December 2, 1988

Donna's driving plans were put on hold until Pathways' completion. But I did take her to parking lots and let her practice in my car. Part of her plans, too, I soon learned, included traveling over the Christmas holidays to see her paternal grandmother, aunts and cousins in Virginia, then on to Connecticut. Going "home" now was especially important to Donna. Her beloved grandfather had passed away at the age of 85 in September, shortly before she left for Mexico. She thought about him often. During one of their last phone conversations, he had said to her, "You sound so good. I can tell by your voice that my old Donna is back." More than anything, she wanted to truly be back with her family and friends for the holidays, and she was.

> *It's 3:30 a.m. and I'm so excited I can't sleep! It is so fantastic for me to be having so much fun all the time again. I thought my depression back in L.A. had to do with the accident, but now I don't think it was depression. I think I was super-lonely. My life has been so blah for almost four years and now it's exciting again. The best thing to help when you're feeling low and inactive is to be around family. It couldn't have been depression because I'm not one to get that way. After all, they used to call me Pollyanna!*

> *Diary, December 12, 1988*

Although Donna was away in Virginia, we talked at least once a day, as always. She sounded terrific as she described her full schedule that included bowling, riding on a tugboat, sightseeing and shopping with her cousin Nancy, Aunt Germaine and friends. She also told me about a bicycle accident she had where she flew over the handlebars and seriously scraped her hands and knees.

She didn't seem too upset about it. In fact it was almost like a badge of courage for her. She was active, busy, doing fun things with people she knew and loved. Her enthusiasm reached such a point at times that it was difficult for me to understand her. "Slow down," I said. "Remember what Rosemary told you."

"I know," she replied. "Slow down and enunciate. I'm trying to be aware and monitor myself when I get tired or excited, but I'll have to try harder. Enunciate, e-nun-ci-ate." She laughed.

One of the many highlights of her visit, she said, was meeting Benjamin Tanner, president of the Virginia Head Injury Group. "He's going to bring me books written by other head injury patients. There are a lot of us around, more than I ever imagined. And so many suffer permanent impairment. I'm so lucky!"

Donna had more than luck going for her. And while she seemed to be continuing in her progression toward the finish line, she did admit to having ongoing short-term memory problems. She still misplaced items, had trouble recalling names (especially those of her young nieces and nephews), and kept "forgetting to remember."

She was learning how to cover her memory lapses, however. "Yesterday, Tommy, my brother, drove me to the mall to do some Christmas shopping," she said. "It was really cold that day and later in the parking lot, I couldn't remember what car we came in or where we had parked. I have less and less reminders of the accident all the time, but that was a real concrete one to me. I didn't tell Tommy because I didn't want him to know. So I just followed him back to the car. I'm sure he didn't spot my confusion at all."

If Donna's schedule was busy in Virginia, it was hectic in Connecticut where she was now welcomed with open arms for the family's Christmas celebration. "This is the first time I've been here since grandpa died," she said by phone one evening, "and I really miss him." I was grateful she had little time to dwell on her loss. She danced, partied, visited longtime friends, and organized albums of old photos for Jean. "I feel good that I can be helpful to Mom in this way. I want to use my time productively," Donna announced proudly. She also joined a group hike to raise funds for a charity, traveled to New York City to see a former colleague from Kodak, toured museums, and ate, ate, ate. "Everyone and everything is so fantastic," she mused. "I'm so glad I made this trip. Being home for Christmas is wonderful." In the next breath, however, she confided that she was telling everyone that she was moving to Virginia.

I'm thinking of moving back here (Virginia) until I go back to work. Life passes you by so quickly and I want to spend as much time as possible with my family. I really want to move here. If Daddy could see me I know he'd be so happy.

Diary, December 16, 1988

I'm having such a great time I want to stay forever. My family is so fantastic. This is just what I needed. Family is so important and my family in Virginia is super.

Diary, December 20, 1988

I told Barbara how I'm thinking of moving to Virginia. She was so excited about it. I'll go back to L.A. as planned on January 4 and move out of my apartment. Barbara pointed out that I've never stayed in one place as long as I have in California. I'm so inspired. I can't believe that things were so dull in my life for such a long time. Now it's time to move on!

Diary, December 23, 1988

Donna returned to Manhattan Beach as planned during the first week in January. She arrived with a smile on her face and loaded with gifts, her Christmas haul and a week's worth of Jean's homecooked specialties for her freezer. I kept waiting to hear more about her plans to relocate as the days passed, but she said nothing. Her only bit of news was that she had met "a super lady" named Flo who organized tours for senior citizens. Florence Legare was well-known in Manhattan

Beach as a likeable, energetic travel coordinator whose slogan was "On the Go with Flo." Hearing "on the go" was all Donna needed.

It wasn't much later that Donna was planning the first of many trips with her new friend, Flo, and a group of area seniors. The 20-day cross-country trip by train had her sky-high with expectations. "I can't wait to go," Donna said. "There's going to be so much for me to do."

Unlike her journey to Mexico when she started off having a good time, her first few days were agonizing. The jiggling movement of the train made it impossible for her to read a magazine or write in her diary. And because her travel-mates were all new to her, she had a difficult time remembering names. "I can't do anything alone," she cried during one of her early nightly calls. "I'm so unhappy. If only you were here. You're my Rock of Gibraltar."

As much as my heart went out to Donna, there was little I could do other than offer words of compassion and encouragement. There was no denying the fear in her voice. She felt trapped in a strange, new environment and I was not two feet away to solve her problem. Perhaps even more distressing for her was the thought that with each passing day, she was moving farther and farther away.

Within several days, however, I began to notice a change in her voice. "This is beginning to work out," she said. "I'm finally getting to know the seniors and they are wonderful, so nice and so patient." The turnabout had not come from anything I had said to her. She had thought it out all on her own.

Seeking companionship, she began to walk up and down the aisles of the train, asking her fellow travelers their names. She was working her brain, stretching her mind, not giving in to her problem but confronting it. She would not be satisfied until she could remember each and every name. One woman in particular continually stumped her. No matter how many times Donna saw this person, she kept drawing a blank. Finally the lady said, "Would it help if I asked you, 'When is your birthday?'"

"That's it," Donna said, gleefully. "Your name is *June!*"

She had done it. Now she could walk the aisles and not only name every person on the tour but feel that she knew them as well. From then on, Donna and the seniors were inseparable, both on the train and off. On other trips, when my schedule permitted, I would fly to a specific location and join Donna and the seniors for the return trip to Manhattan Beach. Donna was so proud to be able to introduce me and say hello to everyone by their first name. Donna felt so close to them. They were like her family.

When the trip ended, she decided to throw a big party in her apartment for the seniors. She mentioned the idea to me and I said, "Sounds like a great idea." At that point that's all I thought it was—an idea. Little did I know that she had already sent invitations to all her new senior friends and the party was that day. She had neglected to do any planning. She somehow thought the party would happen by itself. So Kate and I scrambled around, ordering sandwiches and finger food from the local deli, picking up drinks and cleaning her apartment.

The party was a big success. It was her way of thanking the seniors for making the travel experience her "best yet."

Seeing Donna without stress and anxiety, I knew that I had made a mistake by trying to hold on to her as long as I had. It was alright for her to go out on her own and get bruised a little, I told myself. She was improving by leaps and bounds. Little did we know that there were still big bruises to come.

CHAPTER 11

Donna Grows Up for the Second Time

Donna was in the best shape of her life—physically. Her body was incredibly well toned and defined. At the pool, people marveled at her strong build. In the women's locker room at the Marina City Club, friends and strangers alike complimented her on her figure, and questioned her as to how she maintained it. Wherever she went, her trim, firm silhouette attracted attention.

In five years since the accident, physical fitness had played a major role in Donna's progressive recovery. It was the one thing she knew she could do well, and she used it to help her develop a better mental attitude. She worked out every day, some days more than others, but she never missed an opportunity to exercise. What began as a way to strengthen her weakened leg muscles and pass time soon became her salvation, helping her to stay focused on skills that needed improvement.

As Donna grew stronger and more determined, she began to expand her fitness program, moving from bicycling and walking to swimming, jogging, surfing, weightlifting and aerobics, always under my watchful eye. For several months, tennis too became part of her workout routine. Her instructor was Tracy Austin's sister, Pam, who was very patient and compassionate and was a positive influence on Donna. Donna's days were often strenuous, but she never gave less than her all—and then some.

With Donna almost constantly on the move, keeping up with her, or at least keeping an eye on her, became more and more difficult. Her unsupervised activities—jogging on the beach, walking or wandering about town—became major concerns when she reported an "incident" that had taken place while she was out. A strange man tried to pick her up, wanting her to get in the car with him. Donna knew better than to go with him, but when she refused, he still followed her for several blocks. Her news sent shivers through me. Was the man being overly aggressive, I wanted to know, or were Donna's friendly smile and outgoing personality sending the wrong messages?

Donna should have been angry but she wasn't even offended, she said. She admitted to being ready for a man in her life. "But," she added quickly, "he has to be someone who likes what I like—such as playing sports, being outdoors, being on the go." Hearing her confession made me even more concerned. I strongly cautioned her never to talk to strangers, and to always be on guard with the men she knew.

As it turned out, there were three more negative encounters over a relatively short period, all with respected men in the community, men Donna knew and trusted. One involved a 65-year-old local merchant. It happened around the time of her birthday in June after he invited her to the back of his shop by saying he had "something for her." The "something" came when he pulled her close to give her a French kiss. Shocked and repulsed, Donna pushed him away and ran from his shop, never to return. Another encounter involved a clergyman who came to her apartment "for a pastoral visit." He, too, tried to kiss and caress her against her wishes.

Donna could easily have kept quiet about the incidents, but thankfully, she never hid anything from me. And while they were unfortunate experiences, we both had to face the fact that I could not always protect her from an often unkind world that would try to take advantage of her from time to time. Donna was growing up for the second time in her life. The childlike innocence that was so much a part of her early recovery period had given way to womanhood. This was something I had to face—someday Donna would fall in love and both of us had to be prepared.

Until now, Donna had rebuffed all advances. I could sense a softening of her attitude, however, when she told me that she had met a young man who fulfilled her expectations—he liked being active. I began to think about all of us needing to be hugged and loved. I knew then it was time to have a serious talk with her. So much had developed since the accident regarding the transmission of diseases, and she was completely uninformed. She had to know how to protect herself in more ways than one. With her short-term memory problem, it was a subject that would have to be repeated again and again, I felt certain.

The day of Donna's first date had her sky-high. She was so excited to be going out again, especially with someone who shared her interests. How she looked forward to having fun with the new man in her life. Kate and I were really happy for her. Kate offered to help Donna fix her hair and select just the right clothes and accessories to wear. Donna looked beautiful as she sat nervously awaiting her date's arrival. I was a little apprehensive myself. The man was a stranger to me, and I didn't want Donna leaving without me knowing something about him.

The time for his arrival came and went. We waited in vain for the phone to ring. No one came to the door and no one called. It was obvious Donna's date wasn't going to appear. She was clearly heartbroken, but she said nothing. She simply excused herself and went to bed. I realized that it could have been a miscommunication on Donna's part. I had seen it before. But it didn't change things. For this one time, thank God for her short-term memory. She would hopefully forget this night.

A few days later, one of Donna's closest girlfriends in Manhattan Beach unexpectedly turned on her. They had shared many fun times together over the years before the accident, but the young lady seemed no longer capable of tolerating Donna's erratic behavior or even understanding Donna's inability to fully function in new and unfamiliar environments. Perhaps if she had been open with Donna and told her she was having a hard time adjusting to this new person, then maybe Donna would have understood. As it was, however, Donna was very confused and hurt by her abrupt dismissal, wondering what she did wrong.

Another situation involving one of Donna's therapists followed that unfortunate incident. Rather than praising Donna on her remarkable and continuing improvement, he persisted in not only calling her disabled but telling her that she would never get better. The therapist's hardball tactics lit a raging Irish fire within me. My first encounter with a therapist who had called Donna "history" had me remarkably subdued under the circumstances. This time, however, I stormed into the therapist's office and threatened to disable him. "How would you like to find out what it's like to be challenged?" I shouted. Seeing the fear on his face, I left, slamming the door behind me.

On the drive back to Donna's apartment I blamed myself for turning Donna over to such an insensitive person. Would I never learn? I should have interviewed him first instead of just accepting him as part of the Pathways team. How many other caretakers were naively trusting like me? We must be so very careful when entrusting loved ones to others, I reminded myself. Even doctors don't always know what is best in all cases.

It is so hard to stay positive after all these years. There is no way to stop the pain. The injury is me. It never leaves. I am the accident, the idiot. Enough, God. If you want to test me, OK, but give me a chance. I want to have a normal life.

Diary, March 28, 1990

We did have something to celebrate. On April 8, the fifth anniversary of the accident, I presented Donna with a large trophy of an eagle. On it was inscribed: "You are courageous, fearless, beautiful. You are the wind beneath my wings." From that day on, Donna had two new favorite songs, Bette Midler's "The Wind Beneath My Wings" and James Taylor's "You've Got a Friend."

As close as Donna and I were, things were not going all that well for us. We tried to be supportive of one another, but there were too many times when we were simply at odds. I'd suggest something, she'd disagree. I'd lose my temper, she'd raise her voice. I'd tell her to be quiet. Then we would sit facing each other in painful silence. One day, following a particularly ugly confrontation in the car, I begged Donna to be quiet for three minutes. She suddenly broke the quiet by touching my cheek and saying, "Thank you for being so patient and understanding." She gave me a pass on that one. She knew that wasn't always true. She had just seen me at my very worst, probably the least patient and understanding I had ever been with her. "I know I'm too much of a burden," she added softly. "This must be awful for you."

At times it was. But it was awful for her, too. She was simply telling me she wanted to be normal. She had tried so hard and for so many years—over five long years. The process had gone on long enough!

There was also something she wasn't telling me. I could still hear a determination in her voice. In her own way, she was trying to turn her situation around, trying to work through her problem. Her deep survival skills were at work again. This was one of those dark moments that lead to a brighter time, I told myself. This was another turning point where people either jump ship or stay dedicated. There was no way I was jumping ship. But something had to be done to get Donna back on track. She had reached another crossroad in her progress, and we both knew it.

People began to offer advice, such suggestions as "Keep up the good work and you'll be fine" and "All you have to do to be happy is . . . ." While the thoughts were deeply appreciated, they were only phrases that soon began to take on a hollow ring. I knew what Donna needed more than anything were meaningful activities to fill her day. Her mind needed to be constantly stimulated, which meant she had to be kept busy throughout her waking moments. I became more and more confident that this continual regimen of activity brought her this far and could take her all the way to complete recovery.

The challenge was in coming up with a full schedule for Donna. She already had a fairly good base on which to build. Part of her time was taken up with memory-building therapy sessions. She especially enjoyed working with Rex, the memory specialist I had hired for Donna. He made their sessions fun. To learn the countries and capitals of the world, which she eventually did, he concocted stories that tied the names together for easier learning and recall. It helped that she excelled at the memory games. Always the competitor, Donna loved being the best in her group, wherever she was. From that standpoint, the old Donna was shining through.

She was guaranteed a job in my office for two days a week. Working with other people and the challenge to complete tasks was good for her and I knew it. Donna knew it too. "I have to work or it's just too dull," she told me. "I get so frustrated when I don't have enough to do." While she liked the environment, dressing for it and mingling with her co-workers, the name on the letterhead wasn't Kodak. Even so, she seemed grateful for the chance to pitch in where she was needed despite the fact that her assignments were far below her résumé standards.

Between her therapy sessions and days at the office, she continued vigorously working out on her bicycle, swimming, and taking driving lessons. Not surprisingly, she received high marks from her driving instructor. He told me one day, "She's ready to go out on her own." Not especially good news to me, but Donna was all smiles.

She finally wore me down with her begging, and reluctantly, I said okay to a car. She didn't waste any time in renting one all by herself—a convertible no less—and driving herself to Daniel Freeman for a doctor's appointment. I worried the whole time she was gone, certain this was the resumption of her long-standing love affair with the road. I worried about her left avoidance. I worried about her lack of sense of direction. I worried myself sick, but somehow she made it. I hesitated to ask her any questions.

On the second day of her driving, she was parked in the Bank of America parking lot across from her apartment. She saw me walking toward her and with great excitement she called out "Jimmy!" At the same time she gunned the engine and shot out of the parking lot right into the middle of the street. Luckily it was mid morning with very little traffic and there was no accident, but I went crazy! After that experience she parked the car in the bank parking lot for a week, then returned it without driving again.

She fooled me. Once she proved to herself that she could drive again, her obsession to have a car went away. She was now back to walking or taking a bus. Whether it was out of concern or habit, I can't say, but I was still either trailing her to the bus stop or waiting there for her return whenever she went to the office. It was a good thing I did, too, for there were times when she failed to get off at her stop. If she paid attention to where she was, she was fine. If her mind wandered, however, she kept on going. On one occasion I was waiting for the bus, and as I saw it coming, I stood upon the bench so Donna could see me. As it turned out, it was the day off for the regular bus driver, Ron. As the bus went by, Donna waved and smiled. The next stop was miles away. I jumped in my car, and due to slow California traffic, I was able to quickly catch the bus and wave it over to get her off. Donna found the situation amusing and simply asked, "Jimmy, why are you here?"

On another occasion, I received a call from the principal of El Segundo High School, several miles south of the office, requesting me to pick her up. As a safeguard, we still kept her loaded with identification and phone numbers.

Day by day Donna was becoming more and more independent. However, in searching for "fill-in-activities" to enhance Donna's schedule, one fact kept coming back to me: it was imperative to find stimulating ways to increase her self-esteem. Donna had to feel good about herself to neutralize the negative experiences of people taking advantage of her and the apparent rejection of some of her friends. The activity need not be immediate. An idea, a suggestion, a promise of some future happening worked wonders for her. She loved to look forward to having something to do. Such thoughts filled her with happy anticipation.

I suggested she visit the Manhattan Beach library to sharpen her skills in memorizing world capitals. Not many months earlier she couldn't find the library. Now she not only found it but she made new friends there. After several visits to the library I received a call from Donna asking me to join her. "I want you to meet some people," she said eagerly. I accepted her offer and later told her how proud I was of her. She was creating her own network of friends again.

I also suggested that Donna go to Daniel Freeman Hospital to visit a young woman with a head injury and share her five-year experience with the girl's parents. Donna became an inspiration not only to that family but to others as well. Her visits to the hospital never failed to include a stop to see Sister Jean and Sister Margaret. The look of peace on the nuns' faces always brought contentment to Donna.

The enthusiasm in sharing her recovery with others brought Donna her first speaking engagement. It took place before a large gathering of the Manhattan Beach Welcome Wagon group. Donna loved taking the spotlight to describe how we met, her near-fatal night on the ice, and the differences between right and left brain damage. "The left side of the brain," she explained, "is an important area for speech and memory. There can be permanent damage, but in many cases symptoms can be lessened and even alleviated given the proper care, attention and time." She emphasized the value of a positive mental attitude and patience. Finally, she turned to me, smiled and said, "We're not in a hurry." The audience responded with warm and sustained applause.

That exposure brought Donna a feature write-up in the community newspaper. Having a reporter come out to interview her and take pictures made her feel like a queen for the day. In mid-summer 1987, *The Beach Reporter* headlines read "Miracle in Manhattan–

Woman finds new life downtown on long way back from head injury." It got even better after the article ran. Her phone rang steadily for nearly a week with calls from people who had either suffered a head injury themselves or knew someone who had been in an accident. We heard about young and old and those in between. We heard stories describing falls down stairs, in showers and bathtubs, along the sidewalks and on the beach. A number of injuries came from accidents on bicycles, skateboards and roller blades. We even heard from surfers. The huge response was totally unexpected. If it hadn't been for Donna, I would never have known so many people have been affected. It was then that I began calling the long-term caregivers, the wheel chair pushers, "the silent society."

"You're making people more aware," I told Donna when the calls finally calmed down.

"Let's get in the L.A. Times," she responded quickly. She wasn't joking. She constantly wanted to do better. That's the way she had conducted her whole life, and that was what was driving her now.

As other doors began opening for Donna, she jumped at each opportunity. When she was invited by a local cable channel to make her first television appearance, she didn't think twice, not even about being interviewed by a panel on her recovery process. She found the experience so exhilarating, in fact, that when she had the opportunity to join the cast of a play being presented at Daniel Freeman Hospital, she went full steam ahead. The director of the project was a sensitive young woman named Sandra Bennett. Sandra interacted so beautifully with Donna that I retained her for a time to work with Donna at home. She was very effective in helping Donna get in touch with her feelings, especially her anger.

Good things were happening for Donna at home. She was becoming much more aware of her surroundings, and taking greater pride in keeping her apartment neater. "I'd leave things out all the time," she said, "and never bothered to close drawers or doors. No wonder I couldn't find anything." Finding things without the frustration of having to search for them made Donna less likely to panic. For Donna, keeping her apartment in better order was, at this point, a high level skill, something that could be measured and appreciated. To be told how nice her place looked was like receiving a top grade and became instantly important to her. She was so proud of herself, in fact, that she left a note on her bulletin board. It read: "You'd never guess the person who lives here had a head injury."

Another indication of her new awareness came at the computer. In the time she had been using it, errors had always gone unnoticed. Now she made a point of correcting them. Perhaps it was because her power of concentration was getting stronger. She could sit for longer periods at the computer without becoming restless. She could watch an entire movie on television without becoming sidetracked by other influences. One day I called her from the office because I was running late and wanted to check in with her. "Can I call you back during a commercial? I'm watching a movie," she said. I was shocked. That had never happened before.

We watched the movie *Born on the Fourth of July* together, and one of the hospital scenes with Tom Cruise made a deep impression on her. It must have jolted her memory because she began talking about her experience in the Montana hospital immediately after the accident. "I was in a room with everyone looking down on me," she said. "They were all trying to help, but I didn't know who anyone was."

Another breakthrough came not much later when she awakened from a long nap and remembered everything that had taken place earlier that day. Sleeping had always wiped out her short-term memory. She would wake up and her mind would be blank. "Is it morning or night?" were always her first words.

Then she would ask, "What did we do today?" This time she knew the answer.

All signs of Donna's earlier depression were gone. These were good times for us. She was making, and more importantly remembering, happy memories. Walking to the pier at the end of each day was but one of them. She was not only watching sunsets now, she was recording them in her brain as well as on film. Her photo albums were thick with images of the ever-changing summer sky.

It was a wonderful time for Kate and me, as well. When Donna was happy, I was happy. I always advise people to be responsible for their own happiness and not to turn their happiness over to someone else; but truly, I was happier when Donna was happy. It was a way for me to measure progress. We were so proud of her and all that she had accomplished. The three of us were even beginning to do things together such as going to the Kettle Restaurant— at Donna's invitation. In the past, Donna and I would do things by ourselves or she and Kate would spend time together, but as a threesome, we rarely spent more than a few minutes together. It was awkward and uncomfortable—simple things like, who would walk together since three wouldn't fit across the sidewalk, or who would sit in the front seat while I was driving. Looking back it seems silly, but it was such a delicate situation and feelings were very close to the surface. Now Donna was being more considerate of my needs than her own by acknowledging that she wasn't the only person in my life.

If only Donna's therapists could have seen her as I did, up close on a day-to-day basis, they might have acknowledged her remarkable progress. All the little things that were impossible to detect during random visits were beginning to add up to giant steps forward. The therapists never imagined Donna would be able to dress herself, be responsible for her own hygiene, walk to new places unassisted, be aware of other people's needs, learn new information and retain it, read a book and remember it. But I experienced these miracles every day.

Donna was feeling more confident about herself than she had in recent months. Her self-esteem had reached a new high since the accident. She made more eye contact, held her head up, smiled and laughed more. There was less anger and less talk about her uncertain future. She focused on today and looked to tomorrow. To help keep her progressing, I asked her to travel with me as my "official photographer" during a business trip to scout property at Donner Lake. Donner Estates was a 42-acre parcel of land in Northern California that I was a partner in developing. The scenery in the mountains of Northern California in early fall was spectacular, and Donna clicked her camera at every turn, thrilled to be traveling and working at the same time.

Before we left I told Donna that she would be returning to Los Angeles on her own midway through the trip for a long overdue appointment with Dr. Ludwig. I had tried to reschedule her appointment so she could spend the extra few days with me, but that was impossible. The doctor was booked solid and it was important that she not delay any longer. "No problem," Donna said at the time. "Roy will be at the airport to meet your plane," I had explained. "That's fine," Donna responded, agreeably.

As the time for Donna's departure approached, I reminded her that she would be returning to Los Angeles without me. Her eyes widened and she grew tense. It was as if she were hearing the plan for the first time. "Why are you sending me away?" she demanded to know. "We were having so much fun, and now you want to get rid of me," she said with real anger.

I explained that sending her home was not a spur-of-the-moment decision. We had known all along that she would be leaving early to keep her appointment with Dr. Ludwig. She didn't buy any of it. She had made up her mind that she was in the way, and I was tossing her aside.

Something broke down that day. It was a momentary setback, I told myself. She'd had them before and she would no doubt have them again. But no amount of rationalizing could soothe the pain of her penetrating glare and angry words. Never before had she challenged me so fiercely. After nearly six years of devoting so much of my life and energy to her, how could she believe that I didn't want to be around her anymore?

I returned to Los Angeles several days later wondering how Donna would react to me. Much to my surprise, I needn't have worried. She was all smiles, eager to welcome me back and show me the photos she had taken at Donner Lake. As far as she was concerned, the incident had been completely forgotten. So much of my time and emotional energy had been exhausted on wondering how Donna was doing when, in fact, she had moved on. I was the one who was stuck emotionally in that ugly episode at the lake.

My return, as I soon discovered, wasn't Donna's only reason for happiness. Since we had last seen each other, a young man had come into her life. His name was Pete. An unemployed construction worker and a surfer, they had met at the beach. Pete was teaching Donna how to ride a surfboard, and they were together whenever she had a free moment. After six years of hard work, she was emotionally ready for a romantic companion and longed for someone to care about. She needed someone to share special moments with besides me.

It was easy to tell whenever Donna and Pete were to see each other. With her sense of smell greatly diminished as a result of the accident, and wanting to smell good for Pete, she poured on the perfume. She was going through a bottle a week and complaining, "What's wrong with this stuff? It's weak as water!" It wasn't the perfume. You could smell her a block away. Pete didn't seem to mind, though, and a relationship soon developed. He confessed his love for her and she had the companion she so desperately wanted.

By mid-November 1991, Pete was spending most of his time at Donna's apartment. She was her old self again, busy, having fun, reading books, magazines and watching movies with Pete at her side. To Donna's delight, she didn't have to step foot into the kitchen. Pete willingly did all of the cooking and most of the cleanup. Unfortunately, that was about the height of Pete's ambition. While they shared similar interests such as the outdoors and being active, Pete lacked Donna's determination and drive. He showed no interest at all in looking for work and was content to sit on the beach or in Donna's apartment while she kept her appointments. Still, I felt secure in knowing he was there for Donna—and he made her happy. With Pete in the picture, Kate and I were able to spend more time together. It was the first time we felt comfortable enough to leave Donna and go somewhere together. Kate and I were thrilled to be able to take a short drive up the coast to Malibu for breakfast by ourselves. It was so wonderful to have our life back for a few hours.

Even though Donna told me she had fallen in love with Pete, she was making plans to spend Christmas in Connecticut with her family. Pete was very much against the idea. He wanted her to stay home and be with him over the holidays. I thought she might change her mind when she called me excitedly one morning at 6:00 to ask if I would walk her down the aisle on her wedding day. I swallowed hard and replied, "Nothing could make me more proud." But in my heart I knew he wasn't the right person for her.

However, Pete's proposal did nothing to change Donna's plans, so he began working on her in other ways to get her to stay. A week before her scheduled departure he was out all night with his surfing buddies. Donna was frantic with worry, as Pete hoped she would be, but she didn't back down. Two nights later, he challenged her by threatening to stay with a former girlfriend while she was in Connecticut. He certainly didn't know Donna very well. No amount of coercion could get her to change her mind on this decision. That failing, he asked her to let him stay in her apartment while she was gone. When I heard about his maneuvering, I stepped in with a firm "No way!" His bullying of Donna was beginning to anger me. I felt that if he truly cared for her he wouldn't be playing with her head.

On the afternoon of December 23, Roy Noble and I arrived at Donna's apartment to help her pack and take her to the airport. She was in the bedroom while Pete and his father were sprawled out on the sofa watching television. The sight did not please me. They didn't turn to say hello when we walked in, but I figured they didn't hear us. The sound from the TV was blaring and it was impossible to hear anything. When Pete finally did notice us, there was no reaction. He looked like he had been drinking or he was on something. I suspected at that point that he had a substance abuse problem. I knew I needed to monitor him more closely.

When it was time for Donna to leave she joined us in the living room. She was dressed to travel and she looked wonderful, but Pete made no comment. Nor did he have a Christmas gift for Donna when she handed him his present. He simply got off the sofa, tugged at his father, picked up his clothes and headed for the door. He didn't turn to say good-bye, have a good trip, or even respond when Donna told him he could take her tortilla chips with him. He looked angry, ready to explode. I was grateful we didn't have any trouble with him.

Later that evening, Donna called from a stopover in Chicago and she sounded happy. No mention was made of Pete or his performance prior to her departure.

Ten days later, Donna was back in Los Angeles. Pete met her at the airport and brought her directly to Manhattan Beach. Perhaps Donna's refusal to remain with him over the holidays had made an impact on him. With Donna back in town he acted like a different person. He was kind and considerate and seemed really happy to be with Donna again.

Donna was full of interesting stories about her trip. One especially surprised me. For some reason, she had wanted to visit the convalescent hospital where she was to be sent before I stepped in. "I had to go," she said, "just to see what it was like." She found it depressing. "I never would have made it if I'd stayed there," she went on. "I needed the individual attention and care you gave me." She hugged me and added, "Thank you for bringing me here." On my birthday, January 23, Donna wrote me another of her many beautiful notes. It ended with: "I will see to it you live forever."

Over the next several months, Donna resumed her busy schedule. She continued to enjoy swimming, surfing and her rigorous daily workouts. There were therapy sessions at her apartment with Sandra Bennett, continuing sessions at New Pathways, visits with the nuns at Daniel Freeman, time spent with her senior friends, and two workdays a week at my office. However, these trips to the office were no longer stimulating for her and she said, "It isn't really much of a job."

Fortunately for Donna, Pete became her main focus, taking her mind off her job. In her diary, Donna scribbled: "Love so far, so good." By the end of March, however, I began noticing a change in Pete's behavior and Donna's demeanor. He was growing impatient with Donna, raising his voice and criticizing her for being "absentminded" on occasion. Little things were bothering Donna as well. One evening, Kate and I drove them to a concert in San Pedro, where they visited a piano player who was recovering from a head injury. Donna thought Pete was dressed inappropriately in cutoff jeans and a Hawaiian print shirt and she let him know it. He ignored her. Whenever Donna disapproved of something, she let out a little groan. From that night on she did quite a bit of groaning.

Pete was again acting as he had prior to Christmas—sullen, withdrawn, and temperamental. His actions seemed to have created additional stress for Donna, and as a result, Donna began acting in a confused and disjointed manner. I caught her crossing streets in mid-block, rather than at intersections, and had to caution her time and again about the dangers of jaywalking. We were to meet for breakfast one morning at our favorite restaurant, but she went to the wrong one. She had successfully been paying some of her own bills, but I noticed that her checkbook was a mess and she was constantly overdrawn on her account. I knew she was stressed and I had a strong feeling it was Pete. Because she was growing increasingly tense, experiencing pains in her neck, shoulders and back, I sent her to a local chiropractor, which seemed to help. But that was only a band-aid.

Eventually and reluctantly, Donna told me what was going on. Because Pete practically lived at Donna's apartment, Pete's friends were knocking on her door at all hours of the day and night wanting to party. It was early April 1989, and they had already begun to leave their surfboards on her porch. Several had crashed there for the night and even asked Donna for money. She felt she was losing control of her space and her privacy.

It was never easy for Kate and me to get away, and this time was no exception. Pete's recent behavior concerned me, but I thought he and Donna would work things out and I put Roy in a backup position in my absence.

Kate and I had been planning this special trip to Hawaii for many months. Six weeks after we met, we knew we wanted to be together, but because of my commitment to Donna and concern for her well-being, we waited four years, until now. While in the islands we were married in a small, private ceremony. Wanting to surprise Kate, the morning of our wedding I went outside our hale (thatched hut) and placed beautiful fresh flowers on the grass in the shape of a huge heart. We wore the traditional Hawaiian wedding leis and Kate was adorned with a wreath of orchids on her head. As we exchanged vows, standing inside that heart, our thoughts were only for each other. Our special guests that day were the beautiful Hawaiian children who shared our wedding cake after the ceremony.

A week later on our return to Manhattan Beach, we learned that Pete had created a commotion in the neighborhood when he bashed his truck into a nearby garage. When questioned, he admitted to being on drugs. Donna was heartbroken, but thankful that Pete was not hurt in the accident.

Despite my constant pleading for her to end the relationship or at least have him move out, she refused. He was all she had, she said. We argued over Pete constantly and in one heated exchange I told her that if she continued to have him in her life, I would have to step out. To my devastation, she picked this bum over me.

But approximately six weeks later on May 29, Donna called to tell me that Pete was gone; she had kicked him out. The trouble had started around dinnertime. "It wasn't his drinking, the drugs, or even his antagonism toward me," she said. "He resented my being 'in his face' so much." It was something trivial that brought the situation to a head. Donna had arrived home from an appointment. She was starving, she said, planning on eating a bowl of oatmeal, *her* oatmeal, which she always kept stashed away. But when she went to look for it, it was nowhere to be found. "Pete had eaten it," she said, still angry at the thought. "He ate *my* oatmeal!" It wasn't the worst thing Pete had ever done, but Donna's package of oatmeal was the only thing to eat in the apartment at that particular moment. She had purposely stopped buying food because she knew Pete would eat it all, and he never offered to spend his own money on groceries.

"That was it," Donna said. "That was the end. I screamed at him, 'Get out of here. Get out!'"

I hoped that was the end of Pete. I was grateful that Donna finally realized the kind of person he was and prayed that she would never weaken and allow him back in.

Donna was quick to tell everyone that her relationship with Pete was over. "I let them know when we were going to get married," she said. "Now I have to tell them we're through." To her surprise, she discovered that no one liked Pete anyway. "They all said he was selfish, not supportive, and was taking advantage of me. They all knew that, but they were afraid to tell me. I guess maybe I knew it too, only I didn't want to see it."

Pete may have been out of Donna's apartment, but he was not out of her life. Like a bad penny, he kept turning up unexpectedly, day and night. He was either drunk, on drugs or both. Standing outside Donna's door, he would yell cruel and obscene words to her. At one point he told her the accident never would have happened if she'd known what she was doing on the snowmobile. "It was all your fault, stupid!" he shouted.

Pete's hateful outbursts had a crushing effect on Donna, which had her self-esteem falling to a new low.

ONE MORE SUNSET

She became despondent, frustrated, angry. She snapped at everyone, especially me.

Donna and I were heading for a showdown ourselves. It was impossible to talk with her rationally. No matter what I said, she became argumentative, even hostile. At times she blew up at me with fits of rage and her face reddened as she lashed out. Nothing was right; she complained constantly. Trying to calm her down, I asked her to visualize the customer service department at Sears where "they get paid to listen to complaints." I finally got to the point where I had to tell Donna the complaint window was closed. Because of Donna's remarkable improvements, my commitment was going into its fifth year. But our relationship had come to an impasse and we weren't good for each other any more. I had only one option. I called her mother in Connecticut and said, "Come and get her."

CHAPTER 12

"I Won't Make It Without You"

It was painful and complicated to send Donna back to Connecticut. We had to transfer the conservatorship to her mother which required attorneys and court appeal, but it was something I felt I had to do for Donna's own good. She had to get away from Pete's abuse. The chances of her running into him, or even seeing him again, concerned me greatly, and I didn't think she could avoid him on her own.

It wasn't an easy time for any of us who had been so close to Donna. Not being with her on a daily basis left a big gap in my life. She had been away before, but this felt so final. I missed her smile, her bright eyes, and the way she looked up at me hoping I would fix things for her. I prayed that sending her away would not kill the spirit of the best young person who had ever passed my way.

The many miles that now separated us were made somewhat easier by her frequent phone calls. I heard from her not once but four and five times a day, every day. Her voice was filled with anxiety and pain, and her message was always the same. She was miserable, depressed, bored, and she longed to come back to California. In her mind, I had sent her away because of her affair with Pete. If only she could return, she pleaded. If only I could forgive her.

I'm feeling very low today. I'm so frustrated. I don't have enough to do! It's horrible. I can't get myself involved.

Diary, July 12, 1991

It's so difficult to be in a new environment after having a head injury. I'm having such a tough summer. I haven't really been happy since I left L.A.

Diary, July 15, 1991

I know Jimmy is angry at me because of the way things transpired with Pete. If I hurt him, I'm so sorry. I will never see Pete again. I don't want to see Pete again. Most of all, I don't want to lose Jimmy's friendship.

Diary, July 20, 1991

I wrote Jimmy today to tell him how much I appreciate all he has done for me. I feel so lost without him. I can't believe that he can just drop our whole friendship. I understand that he can't give me all of his time, but I won't require so much time when I get back.

Diary, July 22, 1991

Within weeks of Donna's departure it was obvious that Connecticut had turned into a disaster for her. She wasn't adjusting; nothing seemed to be going right. It tore me apart to hear her begging and sobbing over the phone. I should have been more patient with her, I told myself. I should have been more willing to listen rather than to slam shut the complaint window.

By the end of July I knew I had made a mistake in sending Donna away. She was talking of suicide and saying, "I won't make it without you." Hearing those words had me flashing back to April 1985 at St. Patrick's Hospital in Missoula, Montana. It was there that Dr. Roth had said the very same thing to me: "She will not make it without you."

What could I possibly tell Donna to give her hope, to keep her going? I didn't want to make false promises, yet I had to be supportive and get her mind focused in a positive way. My heart ached for her. It was then that I knew I had to bring Donna back. When I said to Donna, "Be patient and wonderful things will happen," I think she knew it, too.

> *I can't wait to get out of here and return to California. I miss Jimmy. I miss the nuns and the seniors. I miss taking my walks on the walk paths with the Welcome Wagon girls in the mornings. I miss the weather. My beloved Manhattan Beach. I miss it so much!*
>
> *Diary, August 5, 1991*

When Donna left for Connecticut on July 6, I told myself there was no reason to keep her apartment. Something kept me from letting it go, however. Now I was glad I held back. It would be a month, maybe longer, before Donna's return, but her place was still there for her. As luck would have it, I heard about a charming house that was available directly across from Donna's apartment. Without thinking twice, I grabbed it. Finding living quarters at the beach was nearly impossible. To have the listing open up at this time struck me as a good omen.

I had been thinking about relocating to Manhattan Beach since the early days of Donna's recovery. Routinely each morning I drove to Manhattan Beach, parked my car and sat in the Criterion restaurant across from Donna's apartment to wait for her light to go on. The daily back and forth drives from where I lived weren't that far, but the traffic around the Marina, especially during the late afternoon rush hour, was always heavy. The early morning drive was easier but still took time, even at 4:00 a.m. It was during those commutes that I played Napoleon Hill motivational tapes. He was my companion, my motivator. I had been hooked on his philosophy for over 20 years. In the past, I had applied his message to making money. After Donna's injury, however, growing rich had become less important, and I listened from a different point of view. Hill's phrase, "Whatever the mind can conceive and believe, you can make happen," helped direct me throughout Donna's recovery.

Those words came back to me again as Kate and I had our first look at the Manhattan Beach house. We were thinking of starting a family, and as I looked out one of the windows, the town's main street was in clear view. Suddenly I had a vision of Kate and a little girl walking along that street on their way to meet me. Remembering this vision I smiled, when on October 15, 1992, our daughter, Katy Clare, was born. Within a few years my vision had become reality. *Whatever the mind can conceive and believe not only can happen, but does happen.*

Our new home in Manhattan Beach was so perfectly situated that we wasted no time moving in. When I told Donna the news, she sounded happier than I had heard her in a long time.

Jimmy and Kate have moved next door in my Manhattan Beach! It's so exciting to know that we will be neighbors.

Diary, August 8, 1991

On October 3, Donna and her mother boarded a plane for Los Angeles. Before they were even off the ground, Donna was reaching for her diary. She wrote:

It's 10:15 a.m. and I'm finally on my way! I've
wanted to go back to L.A. ever since I got here. This
has been a tremendously difficult time for me. First
of all, I wasn't in a really familiar environment and
I didn't have very many things to do. Some days I
rode a bike that Mom got me to the center of town
(2 miles) to go swimming in the pool at the recre-
ation center. It's real hilly in my area so the bike
ride was tough, and the weather was so hot and
humid. Not many people exercise here. It's a whole
different lifestyle in Connecticut. Mom said she
talked to a doctor who told her that a head injury
always brings on problems. She says my personal-
ity is a lot different, that I'm not as sparkly and
bubbly. I say that's because I've been miserable.
There's nothing to be sparkly and bubbly about. I
think my personality is the same. And if it isn't
now it will be when we get to California!!!

During the three months that Donna had been
away, I heard only trouble in her voice. Now that she
was back everything about her seemed bright, enthusiastic and lively. Only when she talked about her summer of '91 did she appear downcast, but even then
there were fleeting indications of hope. "Whenever I
got really depressed," she recalled, "I remembered
what Roy once told me. He said, 'This too shall pass.' I
repeated those words to myself over and over. As for
Pete: It was a mistake on my part to even associate with
him. His idea of a good time was to go to the beach and
watch the waves come in. I'd be bored in five minutes.
It never dawned on me that he was high on grass. His
being hungry all the time should have been a clue. He
always wanted munchies and he ate my oatmeal!"

The trip to Connecticut didn't get rid of Pete completely. Donna saw him at the beach one day sitting
with a group of his friends. Rather than turning the
other way, she went directly to him and said, "You owe

me big time, you bum! Don't talk to me until you pay back all I spent on you for food and rent."

Surprised, and probably somewhat embarrassed to be told off in front of an audience, Pete replied awkwardly, "As soon as I have some money I'll put it in your mailbox."

"You better!" Donna snapped, glaring at him. Then she turned and walked away. From that day on, she checked her mailbox every time she passed it, but there was never anything from Pete. In fact, she never saw or heard from him again.

Going to the beach was now less important to Donna. She still walked the beach path, but she much preferred a pool for swimming, and so she began searching for available pools in the immediate area. One day while riding her bicycle she discovered the Manhattan Country Club. As Ann Banks, the Club's director of membership, remembered, "Donna wandered in and introduced herself. She told me she had been riding her bike, saw the building and had to stop. Right then I knew she had an inquisitive mind. She seemed so interested, I took her on a tour. It was while we were walking she told me about her accident. Later, as she was about to leave, I took her name and phone number to follow up in case she had any questions. She explained she had a conservator and that he had to make all the decisions. I told her I understood and she left.

"It was months later that Jim came to my office. During the course of our conversation he told me he was the conservator for a girl who had a snowmobile accident. I looked at him and said, 'Donna Jones.'"

Ann's recollection of meeting Donna was still vivid in her mind, and that day I made arrangements for Donna to become a member of the Club. I knew she would be in good hands and the Club's personnel would take special care of her.

"Donna started showing up at the Club at least twice a week," recalled Ann. "We let her park her bike outside the maitre d's office, knowing it would be safe there. We didn't question why she didn't lock it up outside. We just wanted to make things as easy as possible for her."

Donna quickly became an "Esther Williams," outdistancing and out-performing even the hale and hearty male members of the Club. Her endurance was remarkable, and her form had improved to such a point that poolsiders were often absorbed in watching her swim. By now she had mastered her turns. She no longer scraped her fingers at the ends of the pool.

"She was a good, strong swimmer," said Ann Banks. "I believe she enjoyed it at the Club because she found a comfort zone. She had a routine she followed and nice people surrounded her. But then it was easy to like Donna. There was an innocence about her and not a mean-spirited bone in her body. She only saw the positive and we all could take a lesson from that. Her face simply glowed when she spoke."

Ann's big concern was that Donna's outgoing personality and friendliness might be misinterpreted by the men she would meet around the pool. "She was truly interested in people and she wanted to make friends," Ann said.

Donna did meet a man, but not at the Club. His name was Joe and he was introduced to her through her good friend George who owned the local Manhattan Beach laundromat, Whale of a Wash. Everyone liked Joe. He was intelligent, sensitive, caring, a real gentleman always looking out for Donna. On top of all that, he was a terrific softball player. Joe drove Donna to softball games and just about everywhere else, opening new worlds for her. They took in movies, plays, concerts and museums. Her interests and hunger to learn were broadened to such an extent that she began contacting dozens of organizations. As a result, her mailbox was flooded for months with material on everything from whale watching and bird sanctuaries to theatrical events and travel tours. Joe had a remarkable influence on Donna and I considered him a valuable addition to our team. When Joe was in between jobs, I hired him for a time to work in my office.

Donna's adventure with Joe unfortunately came to a halt when a more lucrative opportunity opened up for him in San Diego. Their friendship—and it was strictly that—now had to be continued by phone. And while we all missed Joe, Donna didn't skip a beat. She seemed like the Donna of old, full of energy, spirit, and a newfound independence. If I wasn't available to drive her where she wanted to go, Roy Noble was there for her. And there was always something she had to see and do.

"Donna loved doing things spontaneously," said Roy, "and she would change her mind every five minutes. It was her craving to learn, as if she were making up for lost time."

Donna's craving led her to taking a tour with Flo Legare and a group of seniors, this time through Northern California, Oregon, Washington and British Columbia, where they visited Banff and Lake Louise in the Canadian Rockies. From there they traveled to Calgary in Alberta, arriving during the famous Calgary Stampede celebration. Donna no sooner checked into her hotel than she called me. "I'm so excited to be here now," she said. "It's all hustle and bustle, and everyone is dressed in Western clothes. I just bought a pair of fuschia cowboy boots! I can hear the crowd at the fairgrounds right up the road."

I asked her if she was going there, fully expecting to hear her say yes.

"I really want to go but the group is tired after traveling all day and I don't want to go alone. I'm in a whole different country. If I get lost I won't know where I'm going or how to get back to the hotel."

"I'm sorry you have to miss it," I said.

"So am I, especially when the Stampede is so close. I'm practically there! But you know what? I'm really proud of myself for being able to sort out what I should and shouldn't do. Just to be able to have that much control makes me feel good."

Hearing her say those words filled me with emotion. This was the Donna we'd been waiting for. She had every reason to be proud of herself. I was proud of her too, and I told her so.

"I'm not leaving the hotel," she told me, "but I want to meet some of the people who have come to Calgary for the Stampede. The lobby and lounge are teeming with Canadians."

"Sounds good," I said. "Have fun." It was wonderful to hear the lift in her voice following a disappointment. It wasn't that long ago that she would have been unable to come up with an option, leaving her either depressed or angry.

How Donna would react to the next stop on the tour—Missoula, Montana—worried me. She had seen the town only briefly that tragic day in April 1985, before traveling to the lodge for her ride aboard the snowmobile. If she had any concerns, she hadn't expressed them to me. In fact, she made a point of wanting to visit St. Patrick's Hospital. Knowing how important that was to her, I arranged for transportation to take her from her hotel in Missoula to nearby St. Patrick's.

As it turned out, she had no memories at all of her earlier stay in Montana. "Seeing the hospital felt so strange," she said, calling me immediately following her visit. "I knew I'd been there before but nothing looked familiar, not the building or the people. I didn't remember anything or anyone."

Everyone on the staff certainly remembered Donna, and they made her feel like a star.

"I was walking down the hall," she said, "and I noticed the nurses staring at me. Then I was being mobbed, and people I'd never seen before—or didn't remember—were running up to me saying, 'How are you?' and 'I don't believe it!' One lady even gasped, *'She lives!'* It was amazing. It was like they had turned a spotlight on me."

Donna had such a good time at the hospital, meeting the nurses and attendants who had cared for her while she was in her coma, that she returned the next morning prior to the tour's departure. Dr. Roth, her surgeon, later commented, "It's always fascinating for me to hear about a person who had come in all battered, unconscious and near death, someone I never had a chance to meet. You initially find out what they did for a living and feel that they had a full life. And then to learn about their recovery, to find them doing miraculously better than when you last saw them, is gratifying. It is remarkable what can be accomplished with proper guidance and care. Conversely, it's a known fact that you see less improvement with people who are institutionalized and maintained, but not trained. Donna had good rehabilitation and someone very loyal to her who pushed her and truly wanted the best for her. That's essential.

"One thing that wasn't wiped out in Donna's head was determination. She is a tremendous fighter with good discipline, and even though that was part of her character before, it sometimes disappears with injury. Obviously, it didn't disappear with Donna. To come back as far as she has takes enormous determination on the part of the patient. It also takes tremendous effort and stimulation from a lot of people."

Several days after Donna's return from her travels, we met with Dr. Ludwig at Daniel Freeman Hospital.

He smiled broadly and said to Donna, "You're doing great. Keep up the good work!" Donna returned his smile, then commented, "I only do things that help me get better. If it doesn't work, forget it. I don't even want to look at it."

CHAPTER 13

One More Sunset

The Carondelet Center in the hills of Brentwood, which houses provincial offices and serves as a retreat, meeting facility and retirement home for the Sisters of St. Joseph of Carondelet, opened its doors to Donna in early 1994. She was invited to speak before an audience of nuns about her travels with Kodak and her trips with the seniors.

For many people, standing alone in front of such a distinguished gathering would have been intimidating. Donna never showed any signs of nervousness. She calmly told her stories without missing a beat. Only occasionally, when she became excited in the telling of an anecdote, and she talked too fast, did her words slur. But she was soon back on track, and without notes to rely upon. Never once was she at a loss for words. Her presentation flowed spontaneously—from memory.

When it was all over, Donna received hearty congratulations from the Sisters. With a sly grin, she later remarked to me, "Throughout these past years, you must have wondered when every so often I'd say, 'I'm better now.'" The remark caught me off guard. Had I ever done or said something to make her feel I doubted her progress? Whatever it was had made enough of an impression to remain with her until this special moment. And while I can't deny having "wondered" at times, the feeling was never expressed, I felt certain. After seeing Donna at Carondelet Center, however, any concerns I may have had about her ability to handle herself, especially in stressful situations, were gone. She had proven that to me with her performance.

Within several weeks, we were on our way to South Bend, Indiana. When business takes me east in the fall, I cherish the time in my Notre Dame home at the edge of campus. Although I never had the opportunity to attend Notre Dame, I have long been an avid supporter of the university and its programs. It was in 1986 when I was introduced to head football coach Lou Holtz by then athletic director, Gene Corrigan, that my friendship with coach Holtz began. His philosophy of *Commitment, Trust and Love* was the inspiration for me to continue when times were tough.

Watching the football team was not on my mind now. Donna and I had come to Notre Dame to meet with Rudy Reuttiger, the young man who had triumphed over adversity to play for the Fighting Irish. His inspirational story had been made into a movie, and with its release, Rudy had become a celebrity. When I asked Donna if she would like to meet him, she was practically out the door. She admired Rudy for his determination and gumption. They had a lot in common. Because of my friendship with Rudy, he happily agreed to meet with us.

Donna came away beaming from the meeting with Rudy and she carried with her a large poster from the film. He signed it: "To Donna—Congratulations on your recovery. Keep up the good work. Your friend, Rudy." Donna proudly displays the poster in her living room.

Back in Manhattan Beach, Donna discovered a newfound pride in being able to visualize, an ability that had eluded her for nearly 10 years. She had come back from jogging along the beach and had left her shoes outside on the porch. When she needed them again, she knew exactly where to find them. She could visualize them outside her front door.

214

All of Donna's hard work in therapy sessions, especially with Rex, was finally paying off. Now when she lost or misplaced something, she was able to "see" in her mind where the object was usually kept or where she last had it. No longer did she have to search on and on, growing angrier as the minutes turned into hours, ending only in futility. Her searches had often left her depressed and blaming the accident for every little thing that went wrong. Many times I had to remind her that she would have down days whether she had the accident or not.

Donna's newfound ability was not hit and miss. She was now able to visualize so often and so accurately that she could hardly contain herself. "The right side of my brain has kicked in, at last," she announced proudly. "I don't have to worry about where things are anymore. It makes me feel fantastic!"

Along with her discovery came a bonus: a new order to her life. "Now that my brain is getting more organized, so am I," she said. "I've been messy and disorganized for so long that it was hard to get things done. Suddenly I have a whole new attitude, and it's very exciting." Her new attitude started at home, with straightening and cleaning of her apartment. It wasn't an overnight process. She really dug in, and she was amazed at what she uncovered. There were boxes of coffee filters, dozens of bottles of shampoo and glue, rolls of transparent tape, writing pads, drawers full of blue tights, nail clippers, dozens of menus, weeks worth of newspapers and more. "If I couldn't find something, I'd go out and buy it," she admitted. "Before long I had a warehouse full of things, and I never realized it. Now everything is where it belongs, nice and neat. I never thought I'd say this, but I actually have fun cleaning. My apartment has become so spotless, I feel like I've moved."

With her apartment in order, she filled it with flowers. "I never knew the names of flowers," she said, "so I told myself, 'I have to come up with a way to learn them.'" She did that with the help of her friends Lee and Lisa, owners of the local flower shop, Growing Wild, and their assistant, Scottie. As she bought bunches of flowers, everything from gladiolas, sunflowers and lilies to irises, carnations, peonies and birds of paradise, she became more familiar with them. The names began to stick as she repeatedly saw the filled vases on display in room after room.

The floral arrangements weren't exclusive to Donna's enjoyment. As she became more comfortable in her surroundings, and with her life, she began opening her doors to welcome an increasing number of visitors, not only drop-ins from the beach community but out-of-towners as well. Her mother, Jean, came for an extended stay, followed by her sister, Carolyn ("My pride and joy," as Donna calls her), and longtime friend from Kodak days, Sue Erickson.

Donna met a new friend, Paula Sarcona, while walking along the ocean. "We became friends immediately," recalled Paula, "sharing stories with one another. Donna was so open and friendly. I was fascinated with all she had to say, partly because I have a degree in health and so much of what she told me revolved around the accident. She showed such spirit. There was nothing 'poor me' about her. She was a joy. Great fun to be with."

From that day on, their friendship grew and Paula took an active role in Donna's everyday life. They spent time meeting for lunch, going shopping, organizing her apartment, taking walks and talking on the phone throughout the day. Paula became aware of Donna's need to be busy and feel productive, and so she took Donna with her to community events and continued to look for ways to help Donna feel good about herself. Paula's active role in the community led to Donna's participation in a number of new activities, from charity work to welcoming new Manhattan Beach arrivals through the Newcomers Club. And, thanks to Paula, Donna was appointed official photographer for the local Chamber of Commerce. Paula worked with Donna in this endeavor and they were a great team. Seeing her photos in the local newspaper was a thrill for Donna.

Donna no longer has to search for things to keep her busy. In addition to her other activities, she continues her daily workouts, travels with her mother and the senior groups, adds to her extensive photo collection (she has over 100 albums filled with her photographs), and serves on a newly formed committee at the Carondelet Center with the Sisters of St. Joseph. She even has a long-range project in preparation, one that combines her love of photography and travel: a book of photos that describes how the camera helped her regain her memory. "I used to think, 'What am I going to do now?'" Donna recalls. "I had to work hard to keep things going. Now there aren't enough hours in the day."

Not long ago, I arrived at Donna's apartment to find her taking a break. She was sitting at a table calmly reading a magazine, a cup of coffee at her side. In the background, classical music played softly. All I could see was a poised, beautiful person sitting alone, serene and untroubled. The music wasn't a distraction as it had been only a few years earlier. Nor did my arrival cause her to jump up, run to me and dig her fingers into my back like a frightened animal. Instead, she simply looked up, smiled sweetly, and said, "Hi, Jimmy." That was a sight I wasn't sure I'd ever see again.

People ask me if Donna is the same person she was before the accident. I tell them, "No, she's not the same person. She's better—stronger in every way." I believe that with all my heart. Before the accident, Donna was a terrific person, energetic and full of fun.

But her whole life was wrapped up in her job. Today she's more complete. She's as competitive as ever, but on a different level. Her interests are broader; she's involved in so many activities that earlier held little or no attraction for her. She reads, she writes beautiful letters, she listens to music, she works a computer, she visits libraries and researches a wide range of subjects, she visits museums and galleries, she goes to church. When she tells people of her involvement in these areas, they often respond by saying, "How wonderful. Wish I could do all those things." Donna's reaction is: "Anybody can . . . if they really want to."

How does Donna feel about the person she is today? "If I hadn't had the accident," she says, "I wouldn't have met so many wonderful people. Nor would I have done so many different things that got me from there to here. I could look back and be sad that 10 years were taken from my life, but that's all behind me. I'd much rather look ahead and be happy. I appreciate everything so much more now. I still get frustrated sometimes, but then who doesn't?"

How Donna got from "there to here," as she puts it, is a different matter. She says, "I always felt I had the desire. I wanted to get better and that was it. I also had Jimmy to work with me and guide me. He knew all the buttons to push."

It wasn't me. It was Donna. She had the drive, the ambition, the strong upbeat persona, all remarkably propelled by her injured brain. I believe I was a positive influence in her life and I think that may have helped her recovery time and process. However, being positive before the accident had been her nature, and so perhaps her brain continued to send out positive responses despite the damage it suffered. It is a wonder and a miracle. It also helped to have the right doctor, one who was supportive and open to alternative methods of rehabilitation.

"Despite the nice things Jim and Donna may say about me," says Dr. Ludwig, "I really didn't do all that much. A lot of it was therapy, but it was primarily a combination of Donna's age—she was young—her motivation, luck and the support and care Jim gave her. I was just there to advise and guide them in the right direction. It's not as if I treated her with anything. Donna had enormous strength, both mental and physical, along with a will to live and a reason to go on. If you have those things, chances are you'll make it, and Donna certainly had them. Most importantly, she had Jim at her side and an outstanding team of caring people."

The wonderful feeling that had swept over me on seeing Donna sitting so contently in her apartment was about to return. We were at the airport in Los Angeles and she was ready to board her flight for a visit to Virginia. It was at this same airport, 10 years before, that I had literally carried Donna from a plane with my arms wrapped tightly about her like a straitjacket. She couldn't walk then. She could barely talk, and her memory was almost nonexistent. Now she stood before me looking and feeling glorious, filled with confidence.

As the passengers began to board, she turned and smiled. Her eyes sparkled. Then she was gone. I stood before a huge window and watched as the plane slowly taxied along the runway, then lifted and headed west before circling for its eastward flight. It was late afternoon and the sun was just beginning to set. "We made it, Donna," a voice inside me said. "It's been a long journey, but we finally made it."

Tears streamed down my face as I returned to my car for the drive home. For the first time since the accident, I felt an inner peace in knowing that Donna was safe and strong and confident. It was a feeling that made me want to shout with joy. I still feel that way.

On Donna's return from Virginia, it was clear to me that Donna had embraced our attitude that it's not what happens to you in life, but what you do about it that matters. Confirming this, one evening Donna and her friend Paula were talking and walking along the beach, as they often did. Donna was such a good listener, and as Paula was sharing her apprehension and feelings of insecurity about a new challenge she was about to begin, Donna wanted passionately to help her friend. With the beauty of the sunset behind them, Donna gently put her hand on Paula's shoulder and said with a loud, clear voice, "You can do it. As Jimmy always says, WE DO NOT ENTERTAIN FAILURE!"

EPILOGUE

I
t's a new millenium and it has been 15 years since
Donna's accident. She lives comfortably in her original apartment in Manhattan Beach, overlooking the
magnificent Pacific Ocean. With the help of a few dedicated friends, Donna manages to live on her own and
takes care of herself every day. Although Kate and I
made a permanent move to Notre Dame, Indiana,
Donna is still very much a part of our lives. She shares
many holidays with us, and I continue to visit her regularly on the west coast.

Truly, this story you have just read is a miracle.
When doctors had little hope, I believed in Donna and
her love for life. She beat all odds in terms of regaining
her independence, and today at age 45 Donna lives a
full and rewarding life.

She is in excellent health, walking and running
daily along the beach. She has developed a keen interest in flowers and plants and takes great pride in growing and nurturing her garden. Her enthusiasm for
learning is insatiable and she is an avid reader of books
on an amazing variety of subjects. Donna still visits her
special friends, the Carondelet nuns at Daniel Freeman
Hospital and spends time with the Manhattan Beach
"seniors" every Monday.

According to Donna, her greatest challenges have
been short-term memory, dexterity, sense of direction,
problem-solving and organizational skills. These challenges still exist and she occasionally becomes impatient and angry. However, with determination and
encouragement from her special support team of Paula,
Roy and Betty, her challenges become less aggravating

and more manageable as she finds new ways to compensate. Her self-esteem is steadily rising as she improves every day—learning, reading, growing, retaining and sharing new information—creating new pathways in her brain. Visualization (the ability to form mental visual images), was impossible for Donna after the accident; today, however, this skill is very much in evidence.

I am involved in her life daily, with an average of ten phone calls a day. I have an 800 number and Donna uses it like therapy, leaving messages on my voicemail, just to be able to express her feelings, share her thoughts, knowing they will get to me and I will respond as soon as possible.

Donna enjoys her journey with a wonderful attitude, and with love and guidance I continue to encourage her. I am convinced that my commitment and unconventional approach impacted Donna's recovery significantly in a positive way.

Donna is a beautiful, positive person with a thirst for knowledge and a hunger for life. She is truly blessed to be surrounded by extraordinary friends who include her in their lives because she adds so much to theirs. Today, for Donna, the glass is always half full.